Genre
Screenwriting

2008

The Continuum International Publishing Group Inc
80 Maiden Lane, New York, NY 10038

The Continuum International Publishing Group Ltd
The Tower Building, 11 York Road, London SE1 7NX

www.continuumbooks.com

Printed in the United States of America

Library of Congress Cataloging-in-Publication Data

Duncan, Stephen V., 1949–
   Genre screenwriting : how to write popular screenplays that sell / Stephen V. Duncan.
      p. cm.
   Includes bibliographical references.
   ISBN-13: 978-0-8264-2993-3 (pbk. : alk. paper)
   ISBN-10: 0-8264-2993-9 (pbk. : alk. paper) 1. Motion picture authorship. 2. Film
genres. I. Title.
   PN1996.D83 2008
   808.2'3—dc22
                                                            2008029826

Genre
Screenwriting

How to Write Popular Screenplays That Sell

Stephen V. Duncan

continuum
NEW YORK • LONDON

I dedicate this book to my best friend, Jean, who also happens to be my wife. Without her encouragement, I couldn't do what I do.

About the Author

Steve Duncan is an associate professor and chair of screenwriting at the Loyola Marymount University's School of Film and Television in Los Angeles, California. He is the author of *A Guide to Screenwriting Success: Writing for Film and Television* (Rowman and Littlefield, 2006). His credits include co-creator and executive consultant of the award-winning, critically acclaimed CBS-TV one-hour Vietnam War series *Tour of Duty*; writer-producer of the touted ABC-TV one-hour action series *A Man Called Hawk*; and co-writer of the highly praised Turner Network Television original movie *The Court-Martial of Jackie Robinson*. He has developed and written projects for Warner Bros., Lion's Gate Television, New World Television, vonZerneck-Sertner Films, Spelling Television, Columbia Television, NBC Productions, Republic Pictures, and Tri-Star Pictures.

Contents

4   The Science-Fiction-Fantasy Genre   83

7 Marketing Your Finished Popular Genre Screenplay   135

Introduction

Why Write Popular Film Genres?

There's no need for a drumroll, so let's get right to it: the primary purpose of this book is to provide you with the practical knowledge necessary to successfully deliver the basic elements expected in a popular film genre screenplay—in a word, a commercial screenplay. I realize that in some circles—especially in film schools—the word *commercial* is occasionally considered blasphemous. While art certainly has its place in the world of cinema, all films have commercial value—some more than others—or studios wouldn't produce them, theater chains wouldn't exhibit them and distributors wouldn't sell them to the public in various formats such as the DVD, which is by far the most lucrative vehicle. Then there's the emerging platform of the Internet vis-à-vis downloadable files, which is going to explode once the entertainment industry figures out a stable business model for its use.

So, you write a popular film genre screenplay because they sell and make money for everyone involved.

Expectations & the Unexpected

The people who buy or option screenplays—producers, directors, actors, studio executives—have certain expectations when it comes to what's commercial and what's not. The people who represent screenplays—agents, managers and attorneys—have the job of screening material to match these expectations. As the writer, you must not only deliver on those expectations, but you must also deliver the unexpected: the mysterious essentials of creativity and uniqueness . . . or plain old talent. One factor, among many others, evident with the most successful screenwriters, producers and directors, is the ability to exalt the "rules" of a particular genre to a very high level while managing to bend and even break a few of them along the way. I'm a firm believer in the simple axiom "You can't break the rules until you know them."

So, that's my aim in this genre cookbook of sorts: to furnish you with the recipes for the action-adventure, thriller, science-fiction-fantasy, horror-fantasy and comedy/romantic comedy film genres. You are the chef and must bring to the kitchen the most important factor of all—your talent.

The Drama & Popular Film Genres

The realistic drama you've written can often catch the attention of agents and managers and, perhaps, help you to land professional representation. However, ultimately these reps will want you to write something that they can sell to the entertainment industry, especially to the big studios. Now, don't get me wrong—I'm not saying you shouldn't write dramas. The fact is, the drama is the chassis for all popular film genres.

So, if you're a serious screenwriter who wishes to sustain a career, it's important to be as versatile as your talent permits. Here's a simple testament: the list of produced films between 2000 and 2007 reveals that nearly all fell under the categories of popular genres; few were pure dramas. Realistically, in the long run, dramas do not produce a significant percentage of profits for the industry. Therefore, statistically, it's just plain harder to sell a drama screenplay than one written for mass appeal. Granted, well-written dramas are more likely to collect important accolades—the Academy Award, Drama Desk Awards, Film Festival Prizes, etc.—and that's an essential reason why the larger studios make them. In addition, many dramas find their way to the big screen because an important star or director wants to make the film.

But the bottom line, as they like to say in the biz, is: that unless studios and production companies can keep their doors open, there would be no films produced at all.

Jumpstart Your Writing Career

For now, put aside your drama and begin writing screenplays that will give you a stronger opportunity to start or even resuscitate your writing career. A well-written screenplay in a popular genre is more likely to become a lightning rod for you as a writer. You'll earn clout by demonstrating the ability to generate income (for yourself, your reps and the studios), and in turn you'll gain more value as a writer to help sell your drama script.

When you're the hot writer, it's very common to hear, "What else do you have to show me?"

This Book's Approach

Let me be clear: I do not attempt to probe the deepest psyche of screenwriters and directors of famous or seminal films. Nor do I attempt to analyze the theoretic machinations of films. This is not an academic exercise. I leave that to the Film Studies Doctors of Philosophy. My intention is to give you, the screenwriter, a practical guide to writing each popular film genre—the expected—so that you can add the unexpected: your talent.

This handbook is for screenwriters at all levels, whether a neophyte or someone with screen credits. Because contemporary film genres tend not to be as pure as they were twenty to thirty years ago, I've attempted to isolate the significant elements of each genre category so you can gain the clearest understanding of how to write a commercial screenplay that will snag you an agent or get him or her making phone calls on your behalf.

My approach includes the use of familiar fairy tales such as The Three Little Pigs, Goldilocks and the Three Bears, Little Red Riding Hood and Hansel and Gretel. I apply the elements of each film genre to these well-known stories in order to illustrate the "how to" of each genre.

A Bonus Section: Popular Genres & Television

Because many of the same elements of film genres apply to television, and because television is the single largest employer of screenwriters, I also take a brief walk down memory lane to illustrate how each popular genre has fared on television since the advent of popular series programming in the 1950s.

Let's get started.

1

The Basic Concepts of Dramatic Screenwriting

THERE ARE MANY COMPREHENSIVE BOOKS on the fundamentals of writing a screenplay.[1] However, I want to begin by establishing the broad concepts that are germane and key to my later explanations of how to write popular film genres. My intention is not to be all-inclusive here, but rather to give you a short course in the chief storytelling concepts.

This is important because in order to write strong genre screenplays, you must be able to write a good old fashion *drama*. Look at the drama as the chassis on which to build all the popular film genres: action-adventure, thriller, science-fiction-fantasy, comedy/romantic comedy and horror-fantasy all begin with a strong dramatic framework.

Create an Enticing Film Premise

Nearly every film studio executive will tell you he or she is interested in purchasing screenplays based on a *high-concept premise*. But exactly what does this phrase mean? Basically, in a high-concept premise, *the situation in the premise is more important than the characters in the story*. I will provide specific examples of this in each genre that I discuss because nearly every screenplay written in a popular genre is based on a high-concept premise.

Since moving into the twenty-first century, film studio executives have realized that the "high-concept" approach to screenplay development is getting a bit stale. So they have come up with a new approach to widen their search for unique film premises. The search is now on for what's being called the *low-high-concept premise*. This is a simple variation that takes character into account more than the situation of the story but still relies on a unique situation in which the characters are involved. Essentially, the low-high-concept premise is a *focused* drama. Since actors love drama because it gives them a chance to strut their stuff on screen, this approach has become a way for the studios to help dramas earn more money at the box office. That's a big reason why high-profile-popular actors tend to be involved on the production side of these films, and not just on the screen. Just look at the top drama films made since 2000, and you'll find that the most successful of them involve high-profile actors who also work behind the scenes as directors and/or producers. Two excellent illustrations of this are George Clooney's *Good Night & Good Luck* (2005)—which he co-wrote, acted in and directed—and Clint Eastwood's *Million Dollar Baby* (2004), in which he acted and which he directed. Both of these movies won Academy Awards and made money for the studios. They're both based on low-high-concept premises.

Use Theme in Your Story

What's the story *really* about? What's the big, shiny *idea* underneath the story? Answer this and you'll have the *theme* of the story. If you analyze all the great films, both past and present, you'll find that they all have strong and important themes that are *life-affirming*. What does that mean? Life-affirming themes reassure the audience that their own existence matters. Films, more often than not, offer the audience a chance to go through the perils of life—both physical and emotional—as spectators, allowing them to learn from the experience without the jeopardy. I know that sounds a bit pretentious, but deep down you know it's true when you experience a well-made film.

One technique is to start with a one-word theme that broadly describes what your story is about. An excellent source for a thematic word is *Roget's Thesaurus*. Go to the Table of Contents and look under *Class Eight: Affections*. Of special interest is the section on morality—that's where you'll find the themes most used in storytelling. The struggle between right and wrong—morality—is eternal and universal, because people and films are about people. So this is a natural and very organic approach.

There are other sources of themes, and the most popular are:

- The Seven Deadly Sins
- The Seven Heavenly Virtues

- The Ten Commanders
- Popular Bible Stories

Once you've decided which one-word theme applies to what you want to write, come up with a cliché that would be appropriate for what you're trying to say. Here are few examples:

- *As Good as It Gets:* Trust . . . "No man is an island."
- *Jerry Maguire:* Honesty . . . "Honesty is the best policy."
- *Titanic:* Dishonesty . . . "If you'll lie, you'll steal."
- *Shrek:* Tolerance . . . "Don't judge a book by its cover."

This is the only time when using a cliché is really helpful in creative writing. Otherwise, avoid them.

Next, develop the *physical theme* for your story. This involves giving the audience a clear sense of what the story's main character is up against—a *problem/predicament.* So, if your main character is a police detective, then her physical goal in the story needs to have an underlying theme. In this case, it could be to stop a serial killer who preys only on young women, which is an underlying theme that embraces feminism or the idea that woman are objectified in American culture (and, to be fair, elsewhere on the planet, too).

Next there should be a *metaphysical theme* for your story. This involves the audience in an emotional sensation that underlines a more universal idea in the story, exemplified by the main character's efforts to solve the problem/predicament in which she finds herself. So, following the female police detective, the more universal theme could embrace the idea that women must act on their own behalf in order to level the playing field and not sit around waiting and hoping that men will see the light. Of course, this theme could go in other directions as well.

This theory may strike you as highbrow, but you can easily bring it down to earth by converting both the physical and meta-physical themes into concrete *central questions* that are to be answered (or not) by the story's end.

For example:

Female Police Detective's *physical* central question: *Can she catch the serial killer before he or she kills another young woman?*

Female Police Detective's *metaphysical* central question: *Must women take more control of their lives in order to protect themselves?*

Now let's look at a real-life example of this, using the drama *Brokeback Mountain*, which received an Oscar for Writing–Adapted Screenplay in 2006. (*Brokeback Mountain* also won two more Oscars and was nominated in five other categories[2]):

Ennis' (Heath Ledger) *physical* central question could be: *Can he have a secret homosexual relationship with Jack* (Jake Gyllenhaal) *while maintaining his heterosexual life with his wife?*

Ennis' *metaphysical* central question could be: *Can a person live happily by hiding his or her true self from the ones he or she loves?*

No matter what genre you're writing in, don't forget that theme plays a vital role in the storytelling. It also serves as a guiding light throughout the writing process.

Create Interesting Characters

Stories are, first and foremost, about people. Here's my definition of a screenstory:

> One person with a problem who is trying to solve that problem through other people, and the more other people get involved, the more complicated the problem and its solution become.

Your primary goal as a writer is to create a main character with whom the audience can sympathize. Note that I didn't say *agree with*, because the most important feeling you want the audience to have is that of *understanding* the characters, no matter how they feel or what they do in the story.

One way to accomplish this is to think of the specific role each character plays in the story. The three primary roles are:

Protagonist: Who the story is about; the main character.

Antagonist: The person who opposes the protagonist's efforts.

Pivotal Characters: Those people who help or hinder the protagonist's (and/or antagonist's) efforts and/or bring a different point of view to the story's problem/predicament, regardless of whose side they're on.

Often, new or less-experienced writers consider a protagonist's problem in a story to be the antagonist. For example, you might say that alcoholism is the antagonist. But technically, the love of booze is actually the problem that serves to fuel the kind of behavior that creates conflict in the story. So, in this case, a better way to create an antagonist would be to add a loved one—a wife, girlfriend, brother, doctor—who wants the character to quit drinking, thus opposing the use of alcohol. In this way, you turn the *inner conflict* into an *outer conflict* through a living, breathing person with whom the protagonist interacts. This technique is called personification.

Use Character Triangles

When analyzing most well-written screenplays and films, you'll find that at their core is what I call *character triangles*. There are two basic triangles: one for the mainplot and one for the subplot. Here's a visual representation of the concept.

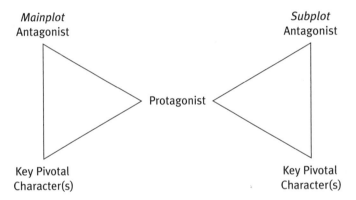

Note that the two triangles are connected by the protagonist. This provides both plots with a strong single point of view. Think of the mainplot as the "public" life of your protagonist—usually the work world—and the subplot as the "private" (emotional) life of your protagonist, usually home or love life. The *physical* central question drives the mainplot while the *metaphysical* central question drives the subplot. In this way, you provide your screenstory with the fuel it needs to drive the through-line narrative.

Develop a Character Arc

This concept means that all your characters—your protagonist, antagonist and key pivotal characters—grow or change over the course of the story. I like to parallel the character arc with Maslow's Hierarchy of Needs. According to that model, our needs start at the bottom and develop in this way:

Self-Actualization

↑

Esteem Needs

↑

Belonging Needs

↑

Safety Needs

↑

Physiological Needs

My version for a character arc goes like this:

Humanity

↑

Community

↑

Family

↑

Bonding

↑

Self

For a full story arc, your protagonist starts out looking out for number one, then meets and bonds with another living thing (a buddy, lover or a dog), resulting in a "family" type of situation (a team, gang, department at work). This inspires the new "family" to become a part of a community (a larger group, like a corporation or country), which strongly motivates the protagonist to pursue a goal larger than him/herself (spiritual in the tradition of Martin Luther King, Mahatma Gandhi and Mother Teresa).

Your characters need not go through the entire five levels of this arc, and it varies from character role to character role. For example, the protagonist may cycle through self, bonding and family, and then stop there, while the antagonist stays, does not arc at all, remaining at self.

Also, this arc could cycle in reverse, with a character starting out at the top of the pyramid, having accomplished humanity, and then spiraling down to being alone and selfish.

Attract Actors & Stars

Stars—above all others—get films made in Hollywood. If not stars, it certainly helps to use recognizable actors in a film. In order to attract stars to your screenplay, you must write roles they will want to play. It's that simple—and that difficult, at the same time. You may find it helpful to have an actor or two in mind for each of the major roles in your screenplay.

Allow the Audience to Be a Character

This is not a trick phrase. It simply means that it's important to involve the audience in your story. By that I mean your screenplay must make 'em laugh, cry, boo or cheer—hopefully all of these emotions. This can happen if you create sympathetic characters with whom the audience can identify, underline their problem—both physically and emotionally—with a strong theme, and make each character three-dimensional.

Create a Love Story

Falling in love is universal. Everyone in the audience has experienced it—whether it's between a young child and a pet, a man and woman, or two close friends. So it's imperative that your screenplay has a strong emotional core—whether it is in the mainplot, subplot or both. You want to take the audience on an emotional roller-coaster ride. That means the relationship(s) are on and off constantly until, by the end, they're either together or not.

Use Suspension of Disbelief

This is one of those concepts you *must* achieve in your screenplay—create a world and characters the audience will believe for a couple of hours. There's no one rule for achieving this. In fact, the only way to get an audience to accept your story's world and characters is to write them convincingly. Generally, this means combining truth with imagination.

Create an Appealing Story & Plot

Let's start with some basic definitions.

Story is *what happens*. Story should focus primarily on the protagonist's emotional wants and needs. Note that there is a distinction between what a person *wants* and what a person *needs*. Often these two goals are at odds, and this can help you to create conflict.

Plot is *how things happen*. A plot is created when the protagonist *acts* on his wants and needs, thus creating *events* in the story.

The binding element for story and plot is often called the *central conflict*. This concept weaves together character arc and theme. Since theme is primarily explored in the subplot relationship, it is there that the protagonist should discover the key to solving the problem in the mainplot, and vice versa. In other words, the protagonist can't fully solve the mainplot problem/predicament without solving the problem/predicament in the subplot. In this way, the two plot problems depend on one another, thus creating a strong narrative through-line.

Use the Seven Elements of a Scene or Sequence

This may fall under the "duh" category because most writers instinctively know these seven elements. However, look at this list as a way to become more authoritative in the planning of a scene (or scene outline), and especially during the screenplay rewriting process.

Here they are:

1. *Protagonist.* This is the character in the scene who has the strongest dramatic need. It can be the story's main character or not. The protagonist in a given scene could be anyone in the story.

2. *Antagonist.* This is the character in the scene who has the strongest opposition to the scene's protagonist. This creates conflict in a scene. Again, the scene's antagonist could be anyone in the story.

3. *Pivotal Character(s).* This is the character or characters who work to keep the scene's protagonist and antagonist in conflict, or provide the scene with a different point of view, or both. This could be anyone in the story, and the character or characters don't even have to be present in the scene.

4. *Dialogue.* This is how the characters communicate, either verbally, non-verbally or both. Because film is primarily a visual medium, you should strive to use non-verbal communication as much as possible.

5. *Intentions.* This is the drive behind each character in the scene. It is the reason why a character is present in a scene. If a character in a scene has no intentions, he or she is a background extra who is there merely to provide atmosphere.

6. *Subtext.* This is what a scene is really about, the scene's undercurrent. Ideally, each scene should embrace a facet of the story's overall theme, whether it supports it or is antithetical to it.

7. *Context.* This is how a particular scene relates to the scenes that have come before it, and how it will relate to the scenes that follow. It is the glue connecting foreshadowing (setups) and payoffs. It is also the thread on which the narrative runs.

Use the Sequence Approach

A sequence is a series of scenes that tell a mini-story within the larger story. In general, films consist of about eight to fourteen sequences. How did I come up with these numbers? I'll explain this in the next section. For now, it's important to understand that many screenwriters use this approach to developing a screenplay. In fact, many writers give clever titles to each sequence so the titles themselves help to tell the larger story. This is similar (but not exactly identical) to the concept of naming chapters on a film's DVD. I've found the chapters on DVDs are hit and miss—some are sequences, but most are not. While DVDs use the chapters as more of a convenience to the consumer, the names still stand as a shining example of how to title your sequences.

A good place to start thinking of sequences is at the story development step of the writing process. This can also be key to the development of your story's structure.

Screenplay Structure: The Classic Approach

When examining the concept of structure, it's often assumed by inexperienced writers that page count defines screenplay structure. This couldn't be further from the truth. Each section's page count—that is, pages 1–10, 11–30, 31–45, 46–60, 61–75, 76–90, 90–95, 96–the end—is the screenplay *pacing*. This is analogous to the way chapters are used to pace a novel or stanzas to pace a poem.

Classic screenplay structure is based on three acts, which mark a beginning, middle and end. This is hardly new, since Aristotle practically invented it.[3] Explaining classic screenplay structure is at the heart of nearly every book on screenwriting, so I won't attempt to do that here. However, here is a stripped-down, basic approach to creating it:

One-to-Two-Page Basic Story (single-spaced). It's here that you should establish the beginning, middle and end.

Five-to-Six-Page Expanded Story (single-spaced). At this step, add detail to the basic one-to-two-pager. A good approach is to write one page each to expand Act One, the first half of Act Two, the second half of Act Two, and Act Three. I like to call these the "four big chunks" of screenplay structure. This is where you should start developing the sequences—mini-stories—that will tell the larger story.

Here are your goals during story expansion.

Act One—Setup

In these thirty pages (minutes), establish the opening sequence (which serves to make a strong promise of the story) and another sequence that leads to the protagonist's problem/predicament. Then make the problem/predicament get worse so the protagonist must act on it. Present the protagonist with a tough moral dilemma—the choice between right and wrong—and use this decision to propel the protagonist into Act Two's "new territory." Act One has at least three sequences, and can have four.

Act Two, First Half—Protagonist Gains Ground

In these thirty pages (minutes), the protagonist should be presented with at least two major obstacles by the antagonist, and should overcome both. In this section of the story, the protagonist gains confidence and skills while frustrating the antagonist's efforts. At the midpoint, the protagonist should encounter a big crisis similar to the moral dilemma encountered at the end of Act One. The decision should propel the protagonist to *prematurely* solve his or her problem/predicament.

Act Two, Second Half—Protagonist Loses Ground

In these thirty pages (minutes), the protagonist is presented with the toughest obstacle he or she has faced so far, but this time the antagonist is the victor. This takes the protagonist to the lowest point, clearly bringing a huge reversal to the story. The antagonist is stronger now, and puts the protagonist on the run and scrambling, eventually causing the protagonist to have only a single option left—confront the antagonist one final time to solve the problem/predicament.

Act Three—Final Confrontation

In these fifteen to twenty pages (note that this "chunk" tends to be a bit shorter than the other three), the protagonist and antagonist have a final face-to-face confrontation called the *climax*. One will win and the other will lose. Then the story ends.

Screenplay Structure: The Alternate Approach

When you hear about *alternative* screenplay structure, it simply means to bend (and sometimes break) the classic rules of storytelling. The most popular choice is not to tell the story in chronological order. This is called *parallel narrative* or *flashback structure*. The basic approach involves alternating the telling of a present story with a past story, jumping back and forth in time. Both stories are related by theme, told through the protagonist's experience, and the key to the protagonist's present problem/predicament is found in the past. These two stories generally collide during (or sometimes before) the climax.

Here's a graphic that illustrates the ideal approach to flashback structure:

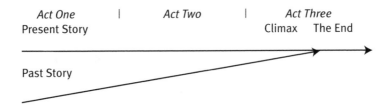

Of course, there are variations to this unconventional approach to screenplay structure.[4]

Use Cinematic Storytelling

The days are long gone when a writer can simply use perfunctory descriptions in a screenplay or master the technical language of movie-making in the script. While a screenplay is not considered literature in the truest sense, establishing tone and atmosphere in a script is paramount to creating a good read.

So, while short stories and novels depend primarily on literary-style prose and can delve deep into the thoughts of characters, screenplays are of a visual nature and must utilize words to paint pictures and rich imagery on the page. It's equally important not to ignore the potential of using sound beyond dialogue in your storytelling.

The easiest way to get inside a character's head in film is through the use of a voice-over. But be careful, as this can become a crutch in your storytelling if overused or misused. Voice-over ideally *adds* to the storytelling, but should not *be* the storytelling in and of itself. A sterling example of this technique can be found in *Forrest Gump* (1994), where the audience gains insight to the protagonist's view of the world using humor, and in *Shawshank Redemption* (also 1994), where the protagonist is the storyteller, taking the audience back to his prison days to explain how he came to be a free man. Morgan Freeman's brilliantly written voice-over is insightful and nothing short of poetic.

Use sound to heighten conflict. For example, if a car is about to hit someone, you could describe the tires "screeching in pain" as the car "hurtles toward the little girl who is frozen in fear." Gunfire can be described visually—"the Beretta spits hot lead"—but sound can bring that to life if you write *"Boom! Boom! Boom!"* Or you can be more subtle—"The wind whips the window shades, banging the glass—Jack sits straight up from his light doze."

The fact that you must write visually does not preclude writing with some literary style. For example, you could write "the two cars pass; their doors scrape" or you could write "the two cars trade paint." This is the difference between a perfunctory action-description and a visual one that adds tone.

To make sure your screenplay is a good read, avoid using camera language as much as possible. In fact, strive not to use it at all. The goal is to pull the reader into your story, and that's much easier to do if you don't remind the reader that it's a screenplay by using technical jargon. The simple guideline is to write what the audience will see on the screen. For example, instead of writing "Long shot of a house on the hill" you could write "In the far distance, the house sits on the hill."

You must strive to write "tight." That means you must make every word count and use as few of them as possible. A general rule of thumb is that an action description should be three lines or less. This creates more "white space" on the page and makes it more inviting to the reader. The days of dense action descriptions are long gone. While grammar and punctuation are important, it's acceptable to bend and even break these rules if it adds tone and atmosphere to your screenplay.

Finally, page format is supremely important for you to master. I like to compare page format to the clothes you wear to a job interview, because first impressions are vital. People who read screenplays as a profession will be instantly turned off if yours doesn't *look* like a script—no matter how brilliantly it's written. While the style of screenplay page format continues to evolve over time—for example, the rules of capitalization have changed over the years—there are still some hard and fast basic rules you must follow. Learn them.[5]

Combine the Rules with the "Visceral" Approach

As a writer, it's important to balance the rules of dramatic writing with your creative instincts. These are not competitive notions; they should work hand-in-glove. No one can teach you how to do this. There are no formulas for how you as a unique individual interpret life and emotions.

But if you look at the successful screenwriters, you'll notice they tend to exalt the basic rules to their highest level, sometimes bending them, but rarely breaking them.

In fact, the finest screenwriters make the rules work in the best interest of their unique talent.

Your Assignment

Use the basic elements of dramatic writing to create commercial genre screenplays.

Notes

1. Among the many books on screenwriting is one of my own: *A Guide to Screenwriting Success: Writing for Film & Television* (Rowman-Littlefield Publishers, Inc., 2006).

2. The 78th Academy Awards nominations by category can be found at *www.oscar.com*.

3. Aristotle's *Poetics* is the primary source attributed to storytelling structure, especially for screenplays. A copy can be readily found for free by searching the World Wide Web.

4. An excellent book on alternative narrative structure is *Screenwriting Updated: New (and Conventional) Ways of Writing for the Screen* by Linda Aronson (Silman-James Press, 2001).

5. There are many screenwriting books that address page format, but one of the best is David Trottier's *The Screenwriters Bible* (Silman-James Press, 2005). Trottier refers to himself as "Dr. Format" and writes a column on the subject for *Scr(i)pt* magazine.

2

Writing the Action-Adventure Genre

Lights! Camera! Action!

```
INT. CYPRESS' AIRBOAT - FLORIDA EVERGLADES - DAY
Roger Chase and Eric True look back as—
Cordero aims the MP5 Submachine Gun—
It spews lead!
They hit the deck as bullets whiz overhead, punch-
ing holes in the airboat's hull!
Cypress jerks the wheel hard—cuts a donut in the
water and heads back directly at Cordero's airboat.
A game of "chicken" unfolds . . .
Shots zip past Cypress as his calm, steady glare
defies a bullet to touch him.

INT. CORDERO'S AIRBOAT - FLORIDA EVERGLADES - DAY
The Seminole Henchman behind the wheel keeps his
course steady . . . as:
Cordero continues to spray lead!

INT. CYPRESS' AIRBOAT - FLORIDA EVERGLADES - DAY
To his great surprise, Cypress catches a bullet in
the arm. He goes down!
The airboat is out of control! Chase grabs the
wheel, steadies the boat as:
```

INT. CORDERO'S AIRBOAT - FLORIDA EVERGLADES - DAY
Cordero runs out of bullets! He shoves the tough
Seminole aside, grabs the wheel.

>   CORDERO
>   Okay, Cubano. It's what I like about
>   you—iron cojones.

INSIDE CYPRESS' AIRBOAT
Chase heads right at Cordero with the same resolve.

INSIDE CORDERO'S AIRBOAT
Cordero holds his course steady—right at Chase.

FROM A HIGH ANGLE LOOKING DOWN
The two airboats, on a high speed collision course, get:
Closer . . .
Even closer . . .
A collision is imminent . . .

INSIDE CORDERO'S AIRBOAT
He chickens out first, cuts his wheel hard.

INSIDE CYPRESS' AIRBOAT
Chase yanks his wheel too, but in the same direc-
tion as Cordero—oh, shi—
Wham! — the airboats slam into each other!!!

I've started with an action sequence from my "spec" (this means written on "speculation," meaning without plans for filming) screenplay *Suicide Chase* to give you an example of action page format, content, tone and writing style. There's also a sense of the key action characters: hero versus villain. There's a chase, and there are guns and violence. This chapter is about how to execute these and other key elements of the action-adventure genre.

Before we go on, it's important for you to gain a basic understanding of the roots of the action-adventure genre. Winston Churchill once said, "Those that fail to learn from history are doomed to repeat it." Here it's not about being doomed, but learning. The goal is figure out a way to re-invent what's been done before, because although there's nothing new under the sun, there are lots of old things we don't know.[1]

Origins of the Action-Adventure Genre

While action-adventure has strong roots in literature, traceable as far back as *Beowulf* (in the first century and believed to be even earlier), the western is arguably the first real action *film* genre. (*Beowulf* was released as a major animated film in 2007 using a twenty-first technology called *motion capture.*) The western is a distinctly American film genre because it embraces the westward expansion of the United States. It depicts the conquest of the wilderness and the subordination of nature in the name of civilization, or the confiscation of the territorial rights of the original inhabitants of the frontier.[2] In short, westerns are about real estate!

We often see this same focus in contemporary action flicks. However, in today's world, the conflicts over homestead, water and gold rights from the Old West give way to wars over oil reserves, mineral deposits (all the stuff that goes into making cell phones and plasma televisions) and homeland security. The preservation of a way of life on the open range now focuses on the effort to spread democracy globally and the clash of diverse religious doctrines. Gunslingers, renegade Indians and swindling town mayors are replaced by serial killers, egomaniacal dictators (and U.S. presidents), suicidal terrorists and corrupt corporate CEOs. And the heroes aren't the squeaky clean, morally superior town sheriffs of yore, but burned-out and morally ambiguous cops and hard-nosed military special operators, like CIA agents, Navy SEALs and Delta Force G.I.s.

The fact is, cowboys, sheriffs, cops and soldiers organically provide the two most important elements of the action-adventure genre: guns and violence. While war is an ongoing staple for storytelling, the western is not. Its popularity tends to come and go. But the *spirit* of the western lives in stories about the present and the future. The action feature film franchise *Star Wars* combines westerns and war seamlessly. The original *Star Trek* action television series (1966–1969) was first pitched to network executives as *Wagon Train* in space.[3] It spawned several spin-offs and is a highly successful feature film franchise.

Some Genre Distinctions

The term *action-adventure* is widely used to label both action and adventure films; however, there are important differences between the two genres.

The Action Genre

Violence—whether with fist, knife or gun—enormous explosions, frenzied car chases and nearly impossible on-foot pursuits are at the heart of today's action flicks. And the action sequence is at the heart of the plot and storytelling. In action films, the hero is generally male (although there are some heroines, in this chapter I'll refer to the hero in the masculine) and gets involved in a predicament he must escape. There's a female involved in some way—sometimes as a love interest, other times as friend. There's a wicked and unrelenting villain. Finally, in its purest state, the action movie tells contemporary stories with specific problems from modern times, and generally does not have consequences for the world at large.[4]

The Adventure Genre

By contrast, adventure films focus on larger-than-life heroes exploring and conquering exotic lands in predicaments linked to greater world conflicts and consequences. Again, the hero is generally male, and there's usually a female who needs rescuing from a perilous predicament. In its purest rendition, the adventure genre embraces stories from history and mythology.

Contemporary Action-Adventure

In films produced in the late twentieth and early twenty-first centuries, the basic elements of these two distinct genres are often combined, thus creating the broader label of *action-adventure*. Regardless, it's important for the screenwriter to understand the differences between the two styles. While the premises, characters, basic story types and plot structure—more often than not—are similar, this knowledge gives you more control over the execution of your screenplay. For the purposes of our discussion, I'll dispense with the distinction between the two genres unless it's appropriate to point out.

Popular Action-Adventure Sub-Genres

Even with the combination of action and adventure, often other film genres contribute to the storytelling to create what's called *sub-genres*. Based on overall box office results, here are some of the most popular.[5]

Action-adventure & science fiction: the *Star Wars* franchise (1977–2005), *The Matrix* trilogy (1999–2003), the *X-Men* franchise (2000–2006) and *Transformers* (2007).

Action-adventure & fantasy: the *Batman* franchise (1966–2008), the *Superman* franchise (1978–2006), the *Lord of the Rings* trilogy (2001–2003) and the *Spiderman* trilogy (2002–2007).

Action-adventure & suspense: the *Die Hard* franchise (1988–2007), the *Mission: Impossible* trilogy (1996–2006) and the *Bourne* trilogy (2002–2007).

Action-adventure & disaster: *Titanic* (1997), *The Perfect Storm* (2000) and *The Day After Tomorrow* (2004).

Action-adventure & martial arts: *Enter the Dragon* (1973), the *Rush Hour* trilogy (1998–2007) and *Shanghai Noon* and *Shanghai Nights* (2000 and 2003).

Action-adventure & heist/caper: *The Usual Suspects* (1995), the *Ocean's Eleven* trilogy (2001–2007) and *The Italian Job* (2003).

Action-adventure & revenge: the *Death Wish* franchise (1974–1994), the *Kill Bill* movies (2003–2004) and *Man on Fire* (2004).

Action-adventure & comedy: the *Rush Hour* franchise (1998–2007), the *Charlie's Angels* movies (2000 and 2003) and *Starksy & Hutch* (2004).

The concept of sub-genres sometimes involves more than two types. For example, the *Pirates of the Caribbean* franchise (2003–2007) brings together action, adventure, fantasy and comedy.

In separate chapters I'll address other popular genres that are often combined with action.

Hollywood's Love Affair with Action-Adventure

Hollywood studios use action-adventure films as the primary source for their *tentpole* movies: big-budget films released during the summer months and marketed to the widest audience possible. This approach puts big bucks into studio coffers.

In the first decade of this century, the price tag to produce the average tentpole action-adventure film is over $100 million, often reaching $200 million. The industry willingly makes this hefty investment because it hopes the bigger and louder action sequences and the expensive, dazzling digital special effects will attract a larger paying audience. If a particular film does very well—and makes a bundle of money—it generally spawns sequels, or even a franchise. The appeal of creating a film franchise is simple: there's a built-in audience, thus marketing is more effective and efficient, and statistically, the odds of making additional profits are higher than releasing a brand new film. Actuarial analysis of the most successful film franchises reveals that sequels garner 50 percent or more of the box office gross of the film that launched the franchise.

Figure 2.1 *Top Box Office Action-Adventure Film Franchises*

In no particular order:

- *Star Wars* (science-fiction-action)
- *Jurassic Park* (science-fiction-action)
- *The Lord of the Rings* (action-fantasy)
- *Harry Potter* (action-fantasy)
- *Die Hard* (action-thriller)
- *James Bond* (action-thriller)
- *The Matrix* (science-fiction-action)
- *Indiana Jones* (action-adventure)
- *Beverly Hills* Cop (action-thriller)
- *Pirates of the Caribbean* (action-adventure-fantasy-comedy)

Choose What to Write

What's comforting about writing genre films is that they're always in demand. No second guessing necessary. To determine what kinds of screenplays sell (or have sold), you need only to look at the films that have top-grossing box office numbers. If you're really ambitious, write a screenplay that has the potential to spawn the next new action-adventure franchise. (See examples in Figure 2.1.) One trick is to come up with a "new" idea. Admittedly, this is hard to do. In 2003, just about no one was expecting a hit movie about pirates. But *Pirates of the Caribbean: Curse of the Black Pearl* pulled in more than $650 million worldwide, thanks to its rousing derring-do, its state-of-the-art wizardry, and Johnny Depp's instantly iconic turn as Jack Sparrow.[6] And trust me, the screenplay written for the first film was crucial to its success.

Another approach is to do what consumer advertising executives call a *gap analysis*: look at what hasn't been made for a while within popular sub-genres—there are websites containing past years' box office results—and write a screenplay to fill that gap.

Screenwriter-novelist William Goldman says "Nobody knows anything" when it comes to being successful in the entertainment business.[7] That's the perfect thing to remember as a screenwriter—we're all playing the odds against success, but your odds improve if you're thinking ahead and taking calculated risks.

Do the Heavy Lifting

The term "heavy lifting" is how writers often describe the process of doing their homework or planning the elements of a screenplay. This section of the chapter presents the elements and concepts you need to figure out in order to write your screenplay.

Action-Adventure & Casting

Who's going to star in your action-adventure screenplay?

The success of the action-adventure genre depends, arguably more than any other, on casting. Some of the classic action stars include Douglas Fairbanks, Errol Flynn, Steve McQueen and John Wayne. Casting these men virtually assured studios that a film would do well financially, even back in those days before the tentpole concept existed.

One wave of action stars in Hollywood includes Sylvester Stallone—*First Blood* (1982) started the *Rambo* franchise; Bruce Willis—*Die Hard* (1988) started the *Die Hard* franchise; Harrison Ford—*Star Wars* (1977) started this and the *Indiana Jones* franchises; and Arnold Schwarzenegger—*The Terminator* (1984) started the *Terminator* franchise.

However, times change—and so do audiences. The twenty-first century has seen a new generation and a new approach to casting action flicks. This is a never-ending trend, because actors come and go and they get older. Today it seems that moviegoers don't associate specific actors with specific genres as they did in earlier times. For now, the trend is moving toward studios casting whoever is the current bankable box office star, whether they're known for action-adventure or not. Tom Cruise earned $100 million for *War of the Worlds* (includes profit participation). Tom Hanks earns $25 million per film. In the $20 million club are Russell Crowe, Brad Pitt, Denzel Washington and Will Smith. Though they have all been in action films, none of these actors are necessarily considered action stars, because their appeal goes well beyond a specific genre.[8] With roles in 2006's Oscar-nominated action-adventure films *The Departed* and *Blood Diamond*, Leonardo DiCaprio is emerging as a fresh choice to cast in an action-adventure film.

As you develop your action-adventure screenplay, envision how the film could be cast. Every major dramatic role is important. If you can imagine a box office star playing not just the hero but other key roles in your screenplay—especially the villain—then you'll have a much better shot at success.

The Most Important Roles to Cast: Heroes & Villains

The American Film Institute (AFI) published a list of the *Top 100 Heroes and Villains in 100 Years*. Among the most popular action-adventure heroes listed are Indiana Jones, James Bond, Ellen Ripley and Superman. The most popular villains are Darth Vader, the Alien, Goldfinger, and the Terminator.

Decide what kind of hero and villain you want to create for your screenplay.

The Hero

There are essentially two brands of heroes: (1) Larger than Life, such as Superman, Batman and Spiderman, and (2) Average Joe, like Neo (*The Matrix*), Luke Skywalker (*Star Wars*) and Ellen Ripley (*Alien*). To help you decide on your brand of hero, let's explore these types a bit:

> The *Larger than Life* hero arrives on the screen ready to fight and to save the world and needs no convincing of it.

> The *Average Joe* hero is unwilling until he has no choice but to save the day.

Regardless of type, it's important to give your hero what's called a *fatal flaw*. Here are some examples to help you:

- Superman—kryptonite
- Batman—fear of bats
- Indiana Jones—fear of snakes (rats, too)

The dramatic importance of the fatal flaw is to create a more human hero, one who is more accessible for the audience.

Give Your Hero a Strong Goal

Plain and simple, the ultimate goal of all heroes is to stop the villain from doing evil.

The Villain

The most entertaining villains are written to be played over-the-top. This character role goes well beyond what's considered the normal thinking and behavior of a real person. Here are some examples:

- Doc Ock (*Spiderman 2*): This guy has iron tentacles coming out of his back!
- Agent Smith (*The Matrix*): He changes into anyone he wants to; oh, and he flies.
- The Joker (*Batman*): Wears heavy makeup and fires off bad puns at his opponents.

Some villains are not human, like the Terminator or a tornado (*Twister*, 1996). But in these cases, the non-human entity is converted into the living so that the audience can identify with the problem on an emotional level: the robot is made to look human by putting flesh on the metal interior and covering him in a biker wardrobe; the tornado is "personified" through Dr. Jonas Miller (Cary Elwes). Note that these particular examples of personification—bikers and corporate lackeys—connote evil.

Make Your Villain Three-Dimensional

Take the time to sketch out the physical, social and psychological profile of the villain (use Appendix A: *Character Development Template*). The more interesting the villain, the stronger potential there is to attract a well-known actor.

Give Your Villain a Strong Goal, Too

Regardless of type, the villain you invent should have a strong goal, just as the hero does. One way to keep the hero and villain locked in battle is to invent a perfect *unity of opposites*. This means that the hero and villain want the same thing in the story. Often, this goal is linked to an object, place or even a person. For example:

- An Object: *Raiders of the Lost Ark*—the ark
- A Place: *The Matrix*—location of the computer
- A Person: *Star Wars*—Princess Leia

Make Your Battle to the Death

Both the hero and villain should want whatever they want badly—for their own reasons—and must be willing to do whatever it takes to get it, including risking death. But remember, in the action-adventure genre, the villain is the active character, while the hero reacts to what the villain is doing. The villain is the catalyst for the action that unfolds in the story and plot.

Heavy Lifting & the Fairytales

To help illustrate how to write the popular genres, I'm going to use three well-known fairytales. They are stories with which you should be familiar. However, if you don't know these stories, I'll tell them to you. You can also check them out for yourself, as they are readily available on the Wide World Web.

For action-adventure, I'm using The Three Little Pigs.

Develop Your Action-Adventure Premise

An action-adventure film tends to be based on a "big" idea. There's a lot at stake for the hero. So, the most appealing action-adventure story idea has the hero saving the world. Note that this is a prime example of how the elements of the two separate genres are combined to blur the differences.

The most successful action-adventure premises fall into the category the entertainment industry calls *high concept*. To review, this means the situation in which the hero (or heroine) finds himself (or herself) is patently more vital to the storytelling than the characters themselves. So, the premise for an action-adventure screenplay should ideally detail a unique or intriguing predicament in order to attract the interest of agents, managers, producers, studio executives and, of course, the audience. Here are three examples of very successful high-concept premises:

- Innocent employees held hostage in a skyscraper by terrorists: *Die Hard* (1988).
- Mankind faces total destruction as a mammoth asteroid hurtles toward earth: *Armageddon* (1998).
- The world is virtual and controlled by a powerful computer: *The Matrix* (1999).

The high-concept premise must be personalized by putting the hero between the unique situation and the villain.

The mere simplicity of the high-concept approach makes it easy to explain, or *pitch*. This also makes it easier for studios to market to audiences. Many who work in the entertainment industry—agents, managers, producers, directors, studio executives—will ask you, "What's the 'one sheet'?" What they want to know is what the movie poster will look like. You should have an idea of this. A good exercise to help your pitch is to write the movie trailer you'd like to see in the theaters and on television. You can do this before or after you finish the screenplay, but you should definitely do it.

The basic premise of The Three Little Pigs fairytale is something like this:

> After a wolf blows down the straw and stick houses of two little pigs and eats them, a third little pig builds a brick house to save himself from the same fate.

How do I translate this into an action-adventure premise?
In this case, I'll start by choosing a hero.
Actually, I don't really have much of choice but to use the third little pig (the one who built the brick house) as my hero, because the first and second were eaten. I'm going to call him John because it's a good American hero name. His last name is Decker because it sounds like a name a tough guy would have. John's goal is to not be "eaten" by the

villain, who is (of course) the wolf. I'm changing "eaten" to "killed" because my movie won't be about cannibalism. Here's my quick thumbnail sketch of the hero:

> *John Decker*, an Army Reserve Sergeant First Class, is an aeronautic technician in civilian life and has just returned to his old job at the National Aeronautics and Space Administration (NASA) after serving back-to-back combat tours of duty in Iraq. He's pissed because he was forced to extend his service commitment past his end-of-duty date. This had a huge effect on his marriage and his relationship with his six-year-old son. Shortly after returning home, his two brothers die in a terrorist attack.

In the fairytale, the villain is the wolf and his goal is to eat (kill) the third pig (after having devoured the first and second pigs). I'm keeping the same name from the fairytale for my villain—*Wolf* has a menacing ring to it—but I'm adding an "e" for style. The villain's first name adds a sense of a superior warrior—ever heard of Alexander the Great? Here's my quick thumbnail sketch:

> *Alexander Wolfe* is a civilian contractor to NASA for the manufacture of rockets that launch military satellites into space. Greed gets the best of him when he's offered millions to help a group of homegrown terrorists send a message to the U.S. government and the American people. He has friends in high places.

Now that I've established a primary conflict for the hero and the villain, I'm going to take this fairytale premise to a more realistic dramatic level for today's adult male audience. The destruction of the three little pigs' houses becomes the destruction of American cities. And the wolf eating two of the little pigs becomes the expenditure of innocent American citizens (metaphorically speaking, the hero's siblings).

Here's my contemporized high-concept premise for The Three Little Pigs:

> An Iraqi war veteran who works for NASA must stop the launch of a series of military satellites that are set to explode and rain down poisonous plutonium over North America, killing millions of people.

Notice that I've taken a contemporary problem and given it worldwide consequences to combine action and adventure elements. As I move forward, I will add more elements to the "heavy lifting" step in the writing process, fleshing out this premise into a story and plot, to demonstrate the development process. But first, I must:

Create a Vibrant Action-Adventure Title

After developing the premise, you need a great title. I personally find it hard to develop a screenplay without one. A title can help you to focus and bring a clear sense of purpose to your writing efforts. Once the screenplay is finished, the title remains a very important element, because it alone can persuade someone to read your screenplay. I've heard of screenplays being purchased just because they had great titles, but this could be an urban legend. Regardless, the challenge is to come up with a title that both has an action-adventure resonance and some-how characterizes what your screenplay is about. Two of the three film examples I'm using here have both qualities: *Die Hard* and *Armageddon*.

My working title for The Three Little Pigs is *Maximum Damage*.

Your title will probably change as you work on your screenplay, and that's okay. The goal is to create a story concept to focus on while developing the major elements and writing the rough draft of your screenplay.

Choose Your Action-Adventure Theme

Action-adventure flicks are about good verses evil. While this simple theme is generally all you need, you can fine-focus it by adding personal emotional stakes for your hero. For example:

- *Armageddon*: Rugged oil-drilling foreman (Bruce Willis) finds his daughter's boyfriend (Ben Affleck) to be the son he never had. *Fine-focused theme: the importance of family.*
- *Die Hard*: a burned-out cop (Bruce Willis) desperately needs to rescue his estranged wife (Bonnie Bedelia) from a violent hostage situation in order to make amends in their marriage. *Fine-focused theme: the importance of family.*
- *The Matrix*: an average man (Keanu Reeves) is told he can save the world from its virtual prison, and he only believes it is possible because of the love of a freedom fighter (Carrie-Ann Moss). *Fine-focused theme: the importance of family.*

It is no coincidence that these successful action-adventure screen-plays incorporate a theme related to family issues and conflicts. This is true because it's necessary to balance the action sequences with emotional relationships. The *Lethal Weapon* franchise is another superb example of this.

A love story is also an important component to include in the high-concept premise. The audience must care about the characters when they're in jeopardy—whether rooting for them or against—for the story to succeed. A love story also serves to make the hero more human, and thus more appealing to the audience.

Your love story can be sexual, it can revolve around family, it can involve a close friend or it can be a combination of these. For many action stories, a close friendship comes in the form of a "buddy" relationship and embraces the idea of male bonding. This works well for the action-adventure genre because the primary audience is male and a significant percentage of the male population has had this experience at one time or another, whether in military service or during organized sports. Even so, it's also wise to include a sexual relationship to make your hero more human for the audience and to help attract the other 50 percent of the population—women. Appealing to the *four quadrants* of marketing—male, female, young and old—is ideal. (More on this in Chapter 7.)

In Film Studies circles, The Three Little Pigs is routinely discussed as a metaphorical representation of the fears and aspirations of the Great Depression.[9] While that may be true (or perhaps over-analyzed), your first priority as screenwriter in the action-adventure genre is to entertain the audience. It's not your job to enlighten the theoretical or demystify the esoteric. We should leave that to documentary films.

My main theme for *Maximum Damage* is genocide. I chose this because in today's world, terrorism is the most dreaded problem, and its goal is to systematically kill racial or cultural groups. To personalize the theme, it's Decker's two brothers who die in a terrorist attack (the family aspect) and this tragedy will spark the need for revenge in the hero (his fatal flaw) who begins to feel that his military service in Iraq was all for naught. I also incorporate tension with his wife and son—father-son conflicts are extremely universal—to further develop a sub-theme of personal sacrifice, which gives the entire story a clear central conflict. This means the audience should understand—whether consciously or unconsciously—that the protagonist can't reach his physical goal in the main-plot unless he solves the emotional conflict in the subplot.

Exploring Morality in Action-Adventure

The hero ideally has the audience on his or her side. He also has a *moral imperative*—a duty and responsibility to uphold the notions of right and wrong. For this reason, it's absolutely necessary for the hero to share the same moral standards as the society at large. In this way, the hero represents the audience in the struggle between good and evil.

In *Maximum Damage*, Decker must uphold the ideal that the right thing to do is to stop terrorism, not just on American soil but across the globe. Of course, he's torn because of his personal tragedy and family conflict and the growing unrest over the war back home.

Morality's Point of View: Exception to the Rule

The anti-hero (or anti-heroine) is essentially a study of evil. This is a simple reversal of a story's point of view. Instead of the audience following the pursuits of the hero, they follow the villain—from his or her point of view. Examples of anti-hero action-adventure films are *Ocean's Eleven*, *The Italian Job* and *The Usual Suspects*—all of which tell their stories from master thieves' point of view. The hero is still an important ingredient to the anti-hero story's conflict, though, as the audience needs someone to root for to stop the villain's dastardly deeds. And sometimes the villain actually reforms and is redeemed in the audience's eyes because of his experiences, such as in action-thriller *Man on Fire* (2004).

Develop Your Action-Adventure Story & Plot

Your story (the primary emotional needs, wants and desires of the hero) should have a beginning, middle and ending—the three acts—and use the key elements of dramatic storytelling (see Chapter 1). However, action-adventure films are plot-driven (as opposed to character-driven), meaning that the story unfolds because of what the hero does about his emotional needs, which are ignited by the actions of the villain.

The Villain's Plan

In the action-adventure genre, the hero's emotional needs are fueled by his moral imperative. Therefore, the most essential element of the action-adventure genre is the villain's plan. This gives the hero his primary goal: to *stop* the villain's plan. The more audacious the plan, the larger the scale the movie can rise to. The villain's crime or conspiracy should have nothing to do with the hero, at least at first.[10] For the screenwriter, an effective approach is to develop the villain's plan independent of the hero. Think of it this way: any character in the story and plot could step forward and save the day, not just your hero. But, of course, it will be your hero who ultimately must do it. The hero is often unwittingly drawn into the villain's plan and becomes a pawn. (See Chapter 3 on thrillers.) This happens because the villain is always superior to the hero in the action-adventure genre. This is an important guideline because a superior opponent forces the hero to go beyond his (or her) normal physical, emotional and intellectual skills to prevent the villain's plan from succeeding. This makes for more suspenseful and action-packed storytelling.

The basic villain's plan in *Maximum Damage* goes something like this:

Alexander Wolfe, a NASA contractor, intends to earn millions of dollars by helping a well-financed terrorist group perpetrate an attack that will make 9/11 pale in comparison. His ultimate terrorist attack is to blow up three satellites at key positions in their orbits, producing a deadly pluto-nium shower over North America. This will result in a pandemic that will kill millions of people in America, Canada and Central America for weeks in the near-term and for years to come.

First, Wolfe must win the bid on the contract. Then he plans to use a series of small terrorist attacks to distract the authorities from his larger conspiracy. Working from within the system—he has operatives at NASA, which includes the Air Force general in charge of the new space military surveillance program, code name "Big Eyes"—he intends to sab-otage the fuel supplies of three of the ten satellites that will launch on the same day, carrying the new ultra-high-tech spy satellites into space.

He will use generous kickbacks for the Air Force general, who has no idea he's taking part in the ultimate terrorist attack on North America, as incentives to control events. Once Wolfe is in control, he'll sabotage three of the ten satellite power supplies, ensure that they're launched into space, and then systematically destroy them when each reaches its planned orbit point.

Wolfe's end-game is to leave evidence of incompetence that points to the Air Force general as the reason behind the satellite program's failure. Wolfe will then disappear and live as a very rich man in the Middle East, protected by the wealthy Muslim extremists who take credit for the attack.

The *Maximum Damage* basic story concept goes like this:

We first meet *John Decker* on his last day in Iraq. He's the first sergeant of an infantry unit and has served back-to-back tours. Shortly after arriving home to his estranged family, a wife and six-year-old son, a terrorist attack on a Miami office building kills his two brothers. In addition to his personal grief, he faces a hard readjustment to civilian life in his job as a rocket technician at NASA, as well as coping with the effects of his absence on his wife and young son, who doesn't really remember him because Decker's been virtually gone for two years. Decker is assigned to the new military satellite surveillance program, code name "Big Eyes."

While working closely with the contractor, Alexander Wolfe, and his boss, an Air Force general, Decker uncovers a lead (he still has friends in military intelligence) to the people who may have been responsible for the attack that killed his brothers. In his lust for revenge (he doesn't trust Homeland Security to do the job), he's unwittingly drawn in and used by Wolfe to sabotage the fuel supply of a series of satellites.

As Decker's family life falls apart, he must undo his misdeed and stop the launches in order to save millions of American citizens from plutonium poisoning. He's able to stop two of the three rocket launches, but the third launch is successful. Now it's a race against time to prevent the planned destruction of the satellite; he must bring it home and disarm the sabotaged fuel supply.

The plot will be the events the hero creates in his efforts to stop the villain's plan.

Develop Your Basic Love Story

The emotional core of the mainplot—the spy satellite terrorism conspiracy—is Decker's need to avenge the deaths of his two brothers. This will develop and unfold as he works to stop the villain's plan. But the heart of the screenplay's love story is the relationship between Decker and his wife, Melanie, and the conflicted anger of his six-year-old son, Danny. Here's the basic love story:

John Decker returns home from Iraq after back-to-back combat tours of duty. Because of the nature of his duty, he hasn't had any physical contact with his wife, *Melanie*, and son, *Danny*, during that time, nor was he allowed to talk about his missions when they communicated via webcam. As soon as Decker reunites with his wife and son, his two brothers are killed in a terrorist attack on the office building in which they work.

Decker becomes more distant because he's obsessed with exacting revenge on those responsible for the attack. Bringing his army buddies back into his life to help him simply pours salt into his marriage's wound. Feeling helpless while Decker is distracted with his vengeance, Melanie and Danny leave Orlando to live with her mother in Miami. When Decker gets close to finding out the identity of the terrorists, his wife and son are kidnapped, and he must rescue them. He does rescue them, and in the process, Melanie gains a new perspective on her husband's anger, and better understands the depth of his sacrifice for his country. Now she's determined not to let his sacrifice consume the ones he loves the most. In the end, Decker and Melanie reconnect, but he realizes it's going to take a bit longer to regain Danny's trust.

Develop Action Sequences & Plot Structure

Most films, especially in the action-adventure genre, tell stories using a series of sequences. By way of review: a sequence is a series of scenes that tell a mini-story within the larger framework of the screenplay's overall story. Think of it as telling your story in chapters. The lengths of sequences vary, and each action sequence contains the same basic elements of a story but in miniaturized form:

1. There's a beginning, middle and end.
2. There's a problem that generates the conflict (action) between the hero and the villain (or a minion) during the sequence.
3. There's something important at stake.[11]
4. The sequence has ups and downs for the hero.

Writing action for action's sake will bore the audience (by the way, your first audience is a reader). The action sequences need to include expressions and explorations of character, not just provide breaks from characterization.[12] That means the audience should learn more about your characters' values (principles), not just their physical capabilities. Choreograph each sequence to create a smaller story (beginning, middle and end) that contributes to the advancement of the unfolding larger story and plot.

Finally, and ideally, each successive action sequence should grow in intensity and magnitude—get bigger and louder—so that the climax is the greatest set-piece. An action set-piece is a set or series of sets in a major location from which an action sequence emanates and unfolds. Here are some examples.

Die Hard uses the building, the offices and their contents, from which to stage action sequences. *Die Hard 2* uses the same approach, with a major U.S. airport standing in for the Nakatomi Tower. Other films imitate this approach. For example: *Die Hard* on a battleship = *Under Siege* (1992), and *Die Hard* on a train = *Under Siege 2: Dark Territory* (1995). *Raiders of the Lost Ark* (1981) uses the exotic locations of northern Africa and Europe where much of World War II was fought. The action sequences in *Ocean's Eleven* (2001) naturally emerge from inside the hotel and casino that are owned by the villain, as well as sur-rounding locales in the city of Las Vegas.

How to Develop "Organic" Action Set-Pieces

First, develop your story with little regard for action set-pieces. Once the story is fleshed out, look at where action scenes can most logically take place and develop your action from those specific locales and situations. In the film *The Rock* (1996), a unique car chase set-piece organically emerges because of the steep hills of the streets in San Francisco. The same type of car chase sequence is also used effectively in the classic action-adventure film *The Getaway* (1972), which is set in the same city and stars Steve McQueen (nothing new under the sun!).

The Matrix is comprised of nine major action sequences (which is about average for action-adventure films). Here are the major action sequences (and set-pieces) from that film.

Act One

1. Trinity's pursuit and escape (the opening sequence). The set-piece is side-by-side abandoned buildings in a dilapidated part of the city.

2. Neo's pursuit by the agents'—lead by Agent Smith—and his rescue by Trinity. The set-piece is Neo's place of work.

Act Two

3. Neo's rebirth and entrance into "reality." The set-piece is going into the "wormhole" and Neo finding himself inside the power supply of the Matrix itself.
4. Neo's training by Morpheus to join the rebels. The set-piece occurs in the freedom fighters' ship and takes place in various locations created in virtual reality.
5. The agents' car pursuit after the glitch in the Matrix. The set-piece is the freeway.
6. Morpheus' rescue and escape from the agents. The set-piece is the agents' headquarters.
7. Neo's fight with the agents in the subway. The set-piece is the abandoned subway station.

Act Three

8. The Sentinels attack the rebel ship. The set-piece is inside the rebel ship.
9. Neo's final battle with the villain, Agent Smith. The set-piece is the abandoned subway station and connecting buildings in the dilapidated part of the city.

Because action is at the heart of this type of storytelling, it's imperative to extrapolate the action potential from "organic" locations and circumstances in your story, *not* to create cool action and force it on the story.

There's a well-known story in Hollywood of how Robert Towne, the screenwriter for *Mission: Impossible II* (2000), had to create the screenstory and write the screenplay *around* the action sequences that the director, John Woo, planned to shoot. Towne—a screenwriter of great experience and skill, who wrote *The Firm* (1993), *Mission: Impossible* (1996) and the classic *Chinatown* (1974)—pulled it off. In my opinion, the film's success is due, in large part, to the love story Towne created between Ethan Hunt (Tom Cruise) and Nyah Nordoff-Hall (Thandie Newton).

Once your basic story works, start building your plot using action sequences—connecting the dots—to bring physical jeopardy to the emotional love story that you've created for the hero. The key here is to first lay out the big events (plot) of the villain's plan, which will create the backbone (or spine) for the screenplay.

I'm going to write my screenplay's rough draft (I actually call this first round a "dog draft" because it's so *ruff-ruff*) around eight major sequences and set-pieces extrapolated from my basic story. Then, as I add detail, I'll create smaller action scenes, such as minor fist fights or scuffles, run and jump escapes or tense arguments, to fortify the storytelling. Here are the major sequences and set-pieces I plan to start with for *Maximum Damage*.

Act One

1. Opening sequence (the "hook"): A terrorist attack on a Miami skyscraper that kills Decker's two brothers, intercut with Decker's last day in Iraq: a suicide bomber attack in the chow hall nearly kills him during breakfast.

2. Decker's car chase through the streets of Orlando (home of the Kennedy Space Center) with one of Wolfe's henchmen ironically ending up on the set of an action movie. The chase is designed by the villain to distract Decker from his job at NASA.

3. Decker's gunfight with Wolfe's henchmen at his apartment, which puts him on what he believes is the trail to his brother's killers (which is also a set-up by the villain).

Act Two

4. Suspected of interfering with their investigation, Decker gets into a shootout at a luxury hotel with FBI agents; Decker steals a fire truck and this turns into a car chase over Key Biscayne Causeway that ends in a gunfight inside a sewage treatment plant.

5. In a big fight and chase through Disneyland, Decker corners the terrorists who he believes are behind the attack that killed his brothers, only to learn that he's being used as a distraction

from the satellite launches. Decker now realizes that Alexander Wolfe is the real villain who had his brothers killed.

The Midpoint

6. Decker goes directly to Wolfe's heavily fortified headquarters and, with a little help from his army friends, nearly destroys the entire campus complex. But Wolfe escapes "by the hair of his chinny-chin-chin."

7. A hot firefight with Decker and the Hostage Rescue Team (HRT) after his wife and son are kidnapped by Wolfe and held in the lower levels of the Predators' stadium, where the local arena football team plays, during the league's annual championship game.

Act Three

8. A low-flying helicopter chase to the Kennedy Space Center to stop the launches. This climaxes in a extensive mano-a-mano showdown between John Decker and Alexander Wolfe on the tarmac at the Kennedy Space Center. But one of the three sabotaged satellites launches and goes into orbit.

9. In a tense ending, Decker brings the satellite back to earth before it reaches a deadly orbit point.

Structure Your Love Story Subplot

Now, I breakup my love story into the three-act structure.

Act One. *John Decker* returns home from Iraq after back-to-back combat tours of duty. Because of the nature of his duty, he's not had contact with his wife, *Melanie*, or son, *Danny*, during that time, nor can he talk to anyone about his missions. Whenever he communicated with his family, it had been tense and cryptic exchanges via webcam. No sooner than their reunion, Decker's two brothers perish in a terrorist attack on the office building in which they work. Decker becomes more distant, as he's possessed with exacting revenge on the attackers.

Act Two. Bringing his Army buddies back into his life to help him simply pours salt into his marriage's wound. Feeling helpless while Decker is distracted with his vengeance, Melanie and Danny leave

Orlando to live with her mother in Miami. When Decker gets close to finding out the identity of the terrorists, his wife and son are kidnapped. He must rescue them.

Act Three. He does rescue them, and in the process, Melanie gains a new perspective on her husband's anger and better understands the depth of his sacrifice for his country. Now, she's determined not to let his sacrifice consume the ones he loves the most. In the end, Decker and Melanie reconnect, but he realizes it's going to take a bit longer to regain Danny's trust.

Create Your Blueprint

The next step is to combine all your elements—the villain's plan, the hero's basic story, the love story and the action sequences—into an expanded story treatment. (See examples in Chapter 4: Science-Fiction-Fantasy.) Maintain the three-act structure and use your wordsmith skills as necessary. Your treatment shouldn't run more than six single-spaced pages. Now you have the blueprint from which you can extrapolate a scene outline.

Once your scenes are fleshed out, you're ready to start writing the rough draft of the screenplay. Or you can create the scene outline while writing the rough draft. For example, you can flesh out each sequence into scenes, then write each before moving to the next.

Key Elements of the Action-Adventure Screenplay

Use Action-Adventure Principal Hallmarks

Stunts. Work to come up with stunts that have never been seen before. Admittedly, this is difficult, so at the very least, create variations of familiar ones. In *The Italian Job* (2003), the requisite car chase is taken to fresh new heights using the unique features of the MINI Cooper, which can operate in narrow places, making a series of car chase stunts the centerpiece for the entire film and integral to the big action-chase climax (not to mention clever product placement). *Star Wars* takes the routine gunfight to a previously unseen level using visually stunning light sabers.

Snappy repartee. It's important to have good back-and-forth banter between characters—whether between the hero and his buddy or between the hero and the villain. This repartee needs to be entertaining, but it also needs to be *functional.* The witty exchanges should accomplish two major dramatic goals: (1) reveal character and (2) advance story. In *Lethal Weapon 4* (1998), Martin Riggs (Mel Gibson) and Roger Murtaugh (Danny Glover) routinely argue over family and personal matters in the midst of gunfights and brutal brawls. While unleashing hot lead on the bad guys, detectives Mike Lowrey (Will Smith) and Marcus Burnett (Martin Lawrence) trade witty barbs in *Bad Boys* (1995) and *Bad Boys II* (2003).

Often, the hero gives the villain a *payback line* during the climax. In *Air Force One* (1997), the president of the United States (Harrison Ford) faces the villain (Gary Oldman) who commandeered his plane. Ford tells him to "Get off of my plane," then sends him out of the plane's tailgate from forty thousand feet. This was set up by the villain telling the hero the plane was his when he first hijacked it.

Here's a bit of snappy repartee from my "spec" action-adventure screenplay *Suicide Chase*:

```
INT. CYPRESS' AIRBOAT - FLORIDA EVERGLADES - DAY
Chase looks down at Cordero in contempt. Then sud-
denly pulls him out of the drink as—
Whoosh—a big gator's jaws booms shut!
But empty! A close call as—
Cordero tumbles into the airboat. As he's catching
his breath, True hovers over him:
                    TRUE
          You're under arrest for assaulting a
          federal officer with a goddamn airboat!
True pulls out his handcuffs, hitches Cordero to
the side of the airboat.
                    CHASE
          The briefcase. Where's the briefcase?
Near panic, they look around—it's underneath
Cordero. True grabs it.
                    TRUE
          Add "attempt to destroy evidence" to
          the list of charges.
```

```
                        CORDERO
        I have the right to an attorney!

                         CHASE
        You also have the right to remain silent.
```

Whack! Chase's heavy boot rings Cordero's bell—he's out cold.

The "ticking clock." This device must provide a sense of urgency for both the hero and villain to achieve their goals. The perfect way to create this urgency is to put deadlines on character objectives—whether it's for the hero or the villain. There should be a clear sense of consequences and impending disaster if the deadlines are not met at a certain time. This is a key ingredient to generating suspense in the story. Here are examples of the "ticking clock" device from the three films I've referenced:

The Matrix: Find "The One" before the Agents do, and destroy him.

Die Hard: Rescue Holly before the terrorists execute the hostages.

Armageddon: Blow up the asteroid before it destroys earth.

In *Maximum Damage* I will use the countdown to the launching of the satellite missiles as the overall "ticking clock." The idea of the hero running out of time creates an organic sense of urgency in the story and plot. Then I will increase the urgency by allowing one of the three rockets to make it into space, because it must be brought back to earth before it reaches a certain orbit point or it will explode.

Combine Action-Adventure with Mythic Structure

In 1949 Joseph Campbell (1904–1987) caused the literary world to stand up and pay attention with his book *The Hero with a Thousand Faces*. This book built on the work of German anthropologist Adolph Bastian (1826–1905), who first proposed the idea that myths from all over the world seem to be built from the same "elementary ideas." Swiss psychiatrist Carl Jung (1875–1961) named these elementary ideas "archetypes," and he believed them to be the building blocks not only of the unconscious mind, but of a *collective unconscious*.[13] Since then, many action-adventure films have utilized the elements of mythology. In fact, Campbell's theory is refined (and made more accessible to the average reader) by Christopher Vogler in his book *The Writer's Journey*, which outlines the three-act screenplay structure in twelve stages:[14]

Act One

- Ordinary World
- Call to Adventure
- Refusal of the Call
- Meeting with the Mentor
- Crossing the First Threshold

Act Two

- Tests, Allies, Enemies
- Approach to the Inmost Cave
- Ordeal
- Reward

Act Three

- The Road Back
- Resurrection
- Return with the Elixir

All stories consist of a few common structural elements found universally in myths, fairytales, dreams and movies. They are known collectively as *the hero's journey*.[15] Campbell's hero's journey is a useful guide for structuring action-adventure screen stories. This approach has influenced such popular action-adventure films as *Star Wars* and *The Matrix*.

Use an Action-Oriented Cinematic Writing Style

Read some already-produced action-adventure screenplays to get a sense of their language and tone. Try to get your hands on early versions of scripts, because they'll showcase the screenwriter's style without studio influence (or interference, depending on where you sit). Read the shooting scripts as well, because you'll be able to gauge how the development process—the seemingly endless suggestions from the producers, director and executives (and sometimes the star)—affect the original draft everyone loved so much at the beginning. Many of the screenplays for films referenced in this chapter can be found on the World Wide Web. Also, many studios publish screenplays in books, and some are occasionally included on the film's DVD release, especially on the newest format, Blu-ray.

Essential Guidelines for Writing Style

Just about every professional action-adventure screenwriter will advise you to:

Use sound. Film, at its best, is a combination of what the audience sees and hears. However, use this technique sparingly or it could become trite. Here's an example:

```
Ka-bam—the airboats collide!!!
```

Or . . .

```
Boom! Boom! Boom! Fire leaps from the barrel of the
SIG Sauer automatic, the hot lead ripping a bloody
hole in the big man's flesh.
```

Use the white space on the page. Avoid writing dense action descriptions. A good guideline is to keep an action description to three lines or less—not sentences, actual lines. Think of it in this way: every time the view on the screen changes for the reader, begin a new action description. Double-space for effect to emphasize important actions on the screen. You could write an action description like this:

```
The Seminole Henchmen sails headfirst into the
drink. So do Cypress and True. Somehow Chase and
Cordero hang on to the steering wheels of the air-
boats. Gators glide toward breakfast: True, Cypress
and the Seminole Henchmen are on the menu.
```

But it's a more effective "read" if you write it like this:

```
The Seminole Henchmen sails headfirst into the drink.
So does Cypress.
Then True.
Somehow Chase and Cordero hang on to the steering
wheels of the airboats.
Humongous gators glide toward breakfast and—
True, Cypress and the Seminole Henchmen are on the
menu.
```

Use simple phrases. Your sentences don't have to be complete. You can use sentence fragments. Here's an example:

```
An Ugly Man with a nasty scar across his face pops
open a manila envelope. He pours out:
```

```
A birth certificate.
A social security card.
A Florida driver's license, and:
A credit card.
The Cloaked Figure picks up the driver's license:
The name is John Smith but the photo is that of:
Roger Chase.
```

Create visual images. The old cliché "show, don't tell" comes to mind. Find ways to get rid of dialogue by converting it to action. Choose words that evoke visual (and emotional) images. It's important to use language to create the right tone and atmosphere appropriate for the story and action-adventure genre. You could write:

CHASE

```
I love you.
```

JENNY

```
I love you, too.
```

Or you could create a more emotionally visual moment like this:

```
Chase looks deep into Jenny's eyes.
There are tears there.
She looks away as a tear rolls down her cheek.
He touches her hand oh-so-gently, offers a loving
smile.
She blinks and smiles back at Chase.
```

Avoid using camera language. It's not your job to direct the film, and you want to avoid reminding the reader that he or she is reading a screenplay. You want to seduce the reader into feeling like the script is the movie—already on the big silver screen. One technique is to use ALL CAPS to replace the camera language. This shorthand is accepted in the industry, but don't overdo it. Here's an example:

```
On the wall:
SEMINOLE ARTIFACTS AND HISTORICAL PHOTOS.
Behind a big desk sits:
Mitchell Cypress with a death stare back at True
and Chase.
```

```
Cypress looks at a SURVEILLANCE PHOTO OF HIMSELF
with JEFF PALMETTO and TWO LOVELY "CASINO BABES."
```

Use active verbs. This helps to create the immediacy of watching a film on the screen while reading the screenplay. Here's an example:

```
Cordero swims for his very life.
Whamp! True wallops the pursuing gator with
the airboat.
Circles around again.
Pulls alongside of Cordero who quickly grabs the
side of the boat.
He's spent.
```

Notice I'm using *active* verbs, such as "swims," "wallops," "circles," "pulls" and "grabs." This brings more life to the tone of the action.

Write tight. Get rid of "and" and "but," replacing them with commas. I call this the "cut and tuck" technique. Also, *avoid words that end with "ing" (gerunds).* A gerund is a verb that has been turned into a noun. In action writing, verbs are stronger. So this goes hand-in-glove with the use of action verbs. Here's an example:

Weak:

```
True is grabbing the wounded Cypress and they are
swimming frantically for the upright airboat . . .
```

Strong:

```
True grabs the wounded Cypress, they swim hard for
the upright airboat . . .
```

Avoid adverbs. Adverbs—words that end in "ly"—are weak. Choose strong verbs to eliminate the need to modify them. Here's an example:

Weak:

```
They swim frantically.
```

Strong:

```
They swim hard.
```

Use mini-sluglines to speed up the read. This is a handy technique to create tension and suspense by eliminating the scene heading elements of EXT. or INT. and time of day designations. This is best utilized when two or more scenes are on a collision course. Don't overdo it; use this only for dramatic purpose. Here's an example:

```
IN CYPRESS' AIRBOAT
Chase determined . . . hits the gas harder.

IN CORDERO'S AIRBOAT
He does the same . . .
Faster . . . Closer . . . Chase jumps out just
before—
Crunch! Twisted metal! Cordero's airboat flips
over! The water drowns the engine.

IN THE SWAMP WATER
Chase realizes he's jumped from the frying pan into
the fire—
Gators cruise in for a feast:
                    CHASE
          Swim!!!
```

Use language to create visual tone. Here's an example:

```
EXT. FLORIDA EVERGLADES - DAY
The airboat skips gracefully across the open dark
waters, speeding back to the civilization waiting
just over the horizon . . .
```

Writing Style Examples from Produced Screenplays

Here's how the pros do it.

George Lucas, Phillip Kaufman and Lawrence Kasdan bring the mythological aura of the ark to life in the screenplay for *Raiders of the Lost Ark* (1981):

```
Inside the Ark of the Covenant is a preview of the
end of the world. A light so bright, a power so
fearsome, a charge so jolting, that there is noth-
ing in our world to compare to it.
```

Jeb Stuart and Steven E. de Souza create an emotional face-to-face meeting of the two heroes in the *Die Hard* (1981) screenplay (an adaptation of Roderick Thorp's novel *Nothing Lasts Forever*):

> The crowd eddies and surges . . . suddenly Powell is
> there, and McClane knows it's him. They stare at
> each other, ten feet apart, and then they're grin-
> ning, extending their hands. But somehow a shake
> isn't enough, and they're embracing each other like
> men who've lived through combat together . . . which,
> in fact, is the truth.

Brian Helgeland crafts a heroic moment in a gunfight in the *Man on Fire* (2004) screenplay (an adaptation of A.J. Quinnell's novel of the same name):

> COP TWO returns fire wildly: the Mercedes is hit
> in a ten-bullet line. Creasy fires two more
> rounds into COP TWO who's hit high in the chest
> and throat. Precise. Creasy pivots, strides calmly
> forward, firing at the men chasing Pita. Boom.
> Boom. Boom!

Figure 2.2 *Writers Guild of America's Greatest Action-Adventure Screenplays*[16]

- *Butch Cassidy and the Sundance Kid*, written by William Goldman
- *Raiders of the Lost Ark*, screenplay by Lawrence Kasdan, story by George Lucas and Phillip Kaufman
- *Back to the Future*, written by Robert Zemeckis and Bob Gale
- *Star Wars*, written by George Lucas
- *High Noon*, screenplay by Carl Foreman, based on the short story "The Tin Star" by John W. Cunningham
- *Patton*, screenstory and screenplay by Francis Ford Coppola and Edmund H. North, based on *A Soldier's Story* by Omar N. Bradley and *Patton: Ordeal and Triumph* by Ladislas Farago
- *The Searchers*, screenplay by Frank S. Nugent, based on the novel by Alan Le May
- *The Wild Bunch*, screenplay by Walon Green and Sam Peckinpah, story by Walon Green and Roy Sickner

---

Action-Adventure & Television Series

There are fewer action-adventure series on television than other genres for good reason—action is expensive to produce. For the most part, television series tend to be either action-drama or action-suspense. This is necessary in order to control production costs. The thing to remember about writing action for TV is to keep sequences contained and short. Most series strictly control the number of action sequences in each episode, so it's important to study the series if you plan to write a "spec" teleplay for it.

Because this is the first chapter on genres—I'll address how each popular genre fared on television in each chapter—here's a brief history of television in the United States.

A Brief History of Television Programming[17]

The earliest television networks in the United States (NBC, CBS, ABC and DuMont) were actually a part of the larger radio network systems, and many of the early television shows were simulcasts of popular radio shows. In 1951, ABC merged with United Paramount Theaters, gaining sizable financial resources with which to compete in a fierce television market. DuMont was unable to survive and by 1956 was no longer viable, with ABC picking up many of DuMont's affiliate stations. Networks offered centralized sales, distribution and production services which lowered costs for individual affiliates. This system was geared toward generating advertising revenue as well, because advertisers were interested in the ability to reach nationwide audiences. During the first five years of the 1950s, ownership of televisions skyrocketed, affecting other forms of entertainment available to the public. This time period witnessed, for example, the closing of many movie theaters, as motion pictures competed with television for consumer attention.

Action-Adventure on TV[18]

To get an idea of how the action-adventure genre plays on television, here's a brief, decade-by-decade walk down memory lane.

In the 1950s, the first action-adventure series on television was the western *Lone Ranger* (1949–1957). The western dominated television in its first decade with such popular series as the long-running *Gunsmoke* (1955–1975), *Wagon Train* (1957–1965) and *Bonanza* (1959–1973).

In the 1960s, the western was gradually replaced by crime-solving series such as *The Wild Wild West* (1965–1969), *Mission: Impossible* (1966–1973, remade 1988–1990) and the long-running *Hawaii Five-O* (1968–1980).

The 1970s took a turn toward the martial arts with *Kung Fu* (1972–1975), which was actually a western. In addition, Michael Douglas stepped out of the shadow of his famous father, Kirk, and became a star on the police series *Streets of San Francisco* (1972–1977), and *Charlie's Angels* (1976–1981) saw the rise of the heroine on television.

In the 1980s, the big hits were *The A-Team* (1983–1987), *Airwolf* (1984–1986) and *MacGyver* (1985–1992), which all focused on high-tech action crime solving.

In the 1990s, martial arts continued its popularity, but this time in a more contemporary western setting, with *Walker, Texas Ranger* (1993–2001). This decade also presented a new kind of heroine in the overtly feminist-themed series *Xena: Warrior Princess* (1995–2001). The macho answer to Xena was *Hercules: The Legendary Journeys* (1995–1999).

Moving into the twenty-first century, popular action-adventure series include *Alias* (2001–2006), *24* (2001–present), *The Shield* (2002–present), *Navy NCIS* (2003–present), *Prison Break* (2005–present), *The Unit* (2006–present) and *Burn Notice* (2007–present).

If you're interested in writing for television, learn how to do it.[19] It's a different art form than the feature film, but the same basic elements of writing an action-adventure do apply.

Your Assignment

Your mission, if you choose to accept it, is to develop an action-adventure screenplay and write the rough draft. But unlike the challenges handed to Ethan Hunt by Mr. Phelps (in the *Mission: Impossible* franchise), I'm offering you a mission that's very doable. To aid your efforts, use Appendix B: *Action-Adventure Worksheet*.

This message will self-destruct in ten seconds.

Good luck and good writing!

NOTES

1. Quoted from Ambrose Bierce's *The Devil's Dictionary*. Bierce was a U.S. author and satirist (1842–1914).

2. Tim Dirks, "Western Films or Westerns," *www.filmsite.org/westernfilms.html* (accessed January 3, 2005).

3. The television series *Wagon Train* was broadcast on NBC from 1957–1962 and then on ABC from 1962–1965.

4. Stuart Voytilla, *Myth and the Movies: Discovering the Myth Structure of 50 Unforgettable Films* (Michael Wiese Productions, 1999), 19.

5. Box office results for films are readily available on the World Wide Web.

6. Josh Rottenberg, "Days of Plunder," *Entertainment Weekly*, May 18, 2007, 29–34.

7. William Goldman's *Adventures in the Screen Trade*, and the sequel, *Which Lie Did I Tell?: More Adventures in the Screen Trade*, are excellent books from which to gain insight into what it's like to be a successful screenwriter working in the entertainment business. Goldman's screen credits span many genres and include such films as *Absolute Power, Misery, The Princess Bride, All the President's Men, The Stepford Wives* and *Butch Cassidy and the Sundance Kid*. He's also a successful novelist.

8. Jennifer Armstrong, Will Bottinick, Scott Brown, Raymond Fiore, Dade Hayes, Jeff Labrecque, Sean O'Heir, Joshua Rich, Missy Schwartz and Alice Lee Tebo, "Are They Worth It?" *Entertainment Weekly*, May 12, 2006, 31–38.

9. Adrian Danks, "Huffing and Puffing about *Three Little Pigs*," *www.sensesofcinema.com/contents/cteq/03/29/3_little_pigs.htm*. (Note: Disney Studios released a very popular nine-minute animated film of the fairytale in 1933.)

10. William C. Martell, *The Secrets of Action Screenwriting* (Studio City, CA: First Strike Productions, 2000), 15–16.

11. Ibid.

12. Jim Cirile, "The Craft of Action," *Creative Screenwriting*, November/December 2004, 58.

13. Kristen Brennan, "Star Wars' Origins—Joseph Cambell and the Hero's Journey," © 1999–2006, part of Jitterbug Fantasia website, *www.moongadget.com* (accessed April 26, 2006).

14. Christopher Vogler, *The Writer's Journey: Mythic Structure for Writers*, 2nd Edition (Studio City, CA: Michael Weise Productions, 1998), 12.

15. Ibid, 1.

16. Source: The Writers Guild of America, West, "The 101 Greatest Screenplays." The list can be found at www.wga.org.

17. Linda Boyd, "Brief History of the Television Industry," *http://scriptorium.lib.duke.edu/adaccess/tv-history.html* (accessed June 11, 2008).

18. Source: *www.tv.com/action-adventure/genre/1/topshows.html&pop=1*.

19. There are many books on television writing, but my book, *A Guide to Screenwriting Success* (Rowman-Littlefield Publishers, Inc., 2006), has a comprehensive section on writing for television, both for the one-hour drama and the half-hour comedy.

Writing the Thriller Genre

A Spine-Tingling Nail-Biter

FADE IN:

INT. CLOSET - BEDROOM - ANGELA'S GOTHIC HOUSE - NIGHT

ANGELA BROWN (22), pretty, washed with innocence in a silky Victoria's Secret nightie, listens hard to the faint SQUEEGEE OF FOOTSTEPS echoing from somewhere in the house.

Cloaked by the shadows, she's terrified. To our surprise—she TURNS DIRECTLY TO CAMERA and breaks the fourth wall with remarkable calm:

> ANGELA
> (whispering)
> Welcome to my nightmare . . .

INT. LIVING ROOM - ANGELA'S GOTHIC HOUSE - NIGHT

Follow a pair of black rubber snow galoshes as:

The INTRUDER—face unseen—skulks through the shadows of the messy restoration of the spacious house . . .

The silhouette of the Intruder stops at the foot of the stairs, looks upward . . .

There's a GUN in the Intruder's black-gloved hand . . .

```
INT. CLOSET - BEDROOM - ANGELA'S GOTHIC HOUSE - NIGHT
```

Angela strains to hear something in the deafening silence. She whispers:

> ANGELA
> Greed and ambition caused this.

The thumps of the FOOTSTEPS draw her attention; they're ascending the stairs, slowly and methodically . . .

Tears flood her crystal blue eyes:

> ANGELA
> I let Mother pull me right into her hideous web of deceit . . .

Finally, a single tear tracks down her pale cheek:

> ANGELA
> It started with a bloody and brutal murder—

```
                                         SLAM CUT TO:
```

The murder: a gluttonous man weighing over three hundred pounds brutally garroted to death from behind by a killer cloaked in black clothes, the executioner's face unseen . . .

This is part of the opening sequence in my "spec" murder mystery-thriller *One Dead Slob, Two Village Idiots & Three Soul Brothers*.[1] The screenplay is a dark comedy in the style of the murder mystery-thriller *Fargo* (1996), written by Joel and Ethan Cohen. While *Fargo* does have brutal violence, it also manages to be ironically funny. Even though a thriller may have comedic qualities (I'll explore the comedy genre in Chapter 6), it still must use the basic thriller elements to achieve the goal of nail-biting entertainment.

The contemporary thriller genre has evolved from three enduring types of storytelling: the murder mystery, the noir and the suspense drama. This chapter will take a separate look at each of them.

First Things First: Key Elements to the Murder Mystery

The murder mystery has been around for a long time. In fact, an account of the *first* murder in the history of the world is in the Bible, in Genesis.

When God approached Cain asking about his brother, Abel—who had been missing for some time—Cain asked, "Am I my brother's keeper?" It turned out that Abel's very own flesh and blood had killed him because of jealousy! The thriller film genre begins with the essence of the crime mystery.

There's a murder. There must be a crime committed, and in the thriller, it's always the worst thing that can happen to a human being: death.

The murderer must be found. Because taking the life of a human being is the worst crime against humanity, the perpetrator must be found.

The murderer must be brought to justice. To confirm the consequences for committing the worst criminal act in society, the perpetrator must be punished.

But there's more to a thriller than these three elements. It's also important for society to discover *why* such a heinous crime has been committed. This moral need embodies two other important elements to the murder mystery plot: truth and justice. These are cherished values in American culture. And then there's revenge. While technically considered morally wrong, revenge is still an important value, and all societies make distinctions between acceptable and unacceptable revenge. This often involves another important moral value: redemption.

Understand Crime Basics

In order for there to be a murder, there must be a dead body, or corpus delicti; otherwise, it's a missing person case, which is fine, but it's not a promise of a murder mystery story. Of course, someone can start out missing, and then the body turns up. Once there's a body, suicide or accidental death must be ruled out. And there must be evidence of foul play.

Forensic evidence is another major element of thriller storytelling. Courts of law require proof in order to arrest and ultimately convict someone of murder. In order for a murder to be proved, there must be three types of evidence:

1. *Motive*: a reason for the murder.
2. *Opportunity*: a reasonable explanation for a suspect to be at the scene of the murder.
3. *Means*: a murder weapon.

A good way to remember these key basic elements is to use the acronym M.O.M.

Understanding and properly using these important elements in your storytelling helps the audience suspend their disbelief. There's nothing more distracting for the audience than getting these things wrong in your story. Once the audience disengages, you're dead, so to speak.

Create a List of Suspects

To make the murder investigation "thrilling," there must be a list of suspects. A suspect is someone who it would be reasonable to think may have committed the crime, possessing one or more of the three types of evidence. Providing the investigator with a list of possible perpetrators encourages the audience to try to guess which one committed the crime. This is a great way to involve the audience in the story.

The Closed Plot Approach

The thrill of the storytelling comes from finding out "whodunit." This approach depends on the pursuit of the unknown; therefore, the thrill for the audience is finding out who committed the crime at the same time that the protagonist does. In the purest thrillers, this revelation happens at the end of the story. One of the best-known films to utilize this type of storytelling is the 1974 screenplay adaptation of Agatha Christie's 1934 novel *Murder on the Orient Express*.

The Open Plot Approach

In this alternate thriller storytelling method, the audience knows—or thinks they know—who did it; the suspense increases as the protagonist pursues the truth. The thrill for the audience includes experiencing how the process of seeking the truth affects the protagonist, and how he or she feels when the truth is confirmed. Playing with an open hand, the suspense writer must create tension by inserting a strong protagonist and developing inventive story developments that avert a certain outcome.[2]

The Closed-Open Plot Approach

The most popular approach in contemporary thrillers is a combination of the two basic approaches. This method first plays on mystery for suspense—the first half of the story is to find out "whodunit"—and then it plays on pursuing justice, as the second half focuses on catching the culprit.

Choose one for your screenplay.

Origins & Key Elements of Noir

After World War II, several concurrent developments marked the creation, definition and popularization of both literary and cinematic noir: the Hollywood production of a growing number of pessimistic, downbeat crime films; the post-war release in Europe of a large backlog of American films; the publication in France of a new series of crime novels; and the appearance in America of a new kind of book, the paperback original. Films released in America just before the end of the war, such as Billy Wilder's *Double Indemnity* and Edward Dmytryk's *Murder, My Sweet* (both 1944), were taken as evidence when they appeared in France that "the Americans are making dark films too."[3]

Often considered to have reinvigorated noir in Hollywood, the film *Chinatown* (1974) set into motion the trend toward *new noir* or *neo-noir*. This approach puts more emphasis on erotic thrills in the storytelling, and has spawned films such as *Taxi Driver* (1976), *Body Heat* (1981), *The Grifters* (1990) and *Basic Instinct* (1992). In the same year that *Basic Instinct* was released, neo-noir took a more graphic, violent turn with Quentin Tarantino's cult hit *Reservoir Dogs*. Other films with stories revolving around brutality followed: *The Usual Suspects* (1995), *Fargo* (1996) and *L.A. Confidential* (1997).

Employ Classic Noir Storytelling Techniques

Exploit betrayal. The noir genre revolves around one character betraying another, or when high-stakes betrayal has nationwide or even worldwide consequences.[4] Betrayal is the key element that drives a noir story and plot.

Use parallel narratives. This means that there are two stories in play: one from the "past," the other in the "present." The narrative embraces the idea that the protagonist's past is catching up to him (or her) and must finally be dealt with, always at a critical time in his or her current life.

Use witty voice-over and dialogue. Providing the audience with a clear insight into the moral dilemmas and emotions faced by the protagonist most often requires the use of the protagonist's voice-over as a storytelling device. The voice-over always reveals the protagonist's sharp wit and gut feelings. Here's an example from the film *Out of the Past* (1947), adapted by Daniel Mainwaring (using the pseudonym Geoffrey Homes) and staring Robert Mitchum as Jeff Bailey. Jeff's idyllic life is interrupted when a gangster he worked for in his past (played menacingly by Kirk Douglas) forces him to find his estranged girlfriend, who has absconded with a great deal of the gangster's money:

> JEFF BAILEY
> You don't get vaccinated for Florida, but you do for Mexico. So I just followed that pounds of excess baggage to Mexico City. She had been at the Reforma and then gone. I took the bus south like she did. It was hot in Taxco. You say to yourself, "How hot can it get?" And then in Acapulco, you find out . . .

Here's a witty retort Sam Spade (Humphrey Bogart) has for Joel Cairo (Peter Lorre) in *The Maltese Falcon* (1941)—written by Dashiell Hammett (novel) and John Huston (screenplay)—which is considered the first noir film:

> SPADE
> You always have a very smooth explanation . . .

> CAIRO
> What you want me to do, learn to stutter?

Create a not-so-happy ending. In most traditional noir stories, the ending is not a good one for the protagonist. Many contemporary noirs ignore this, however, because today's audiences are not thrilled with "bummer" endings.

Create the anticipation of violence. The dramatic tension in newer noir films come from the anticipation of violence, perpetrated by characters with few or no redeeming qualities. Good and evil are sometimes indistinguishable and, on a thematic level, evil represents a frightening, dark side of ourselves. These types of stories are compelling to watch because they deliver the thrill of danger without the risk of consequences.

Use a femme fatale. This character role is a symbol of a better life for the protagonist. Usually she's wealthy, intelligent and illusive, and the protagonist lusts for and obsesses about her. But the femme fatale uses him for her own agenda (a key component of the betrayal factor) and, in the end, deceives him. Prime examples are Catherine Tramell (Sharon Stone) in *Basic Instinct* and Lynn Bracken (Kim Bassinger, who won an Oscar for this portrayal) in *L.A. Confidential.*

Create a visually dark atmosphere. Noir stories mostly take place in lonely bars, seedy motels, dark rooms and abandoned, shadowy, wet streets. These locations are used to suggest isolation and fear, and to warn the audience of impending violence.

Figure 3.1   *Classic Noir Films*

You should screen and analyze these classics:

- *Notorious* (1946)
- *The Postman Always Rings Twice* (1946)
- *Out of the Past* (1947)
- *The Asphalt Jungle* (1950)

Origins & Key Elements of Suspense Drama

Film director Alfred Hitchcock—known as the "master of suspense"—captures the darkest fears of the audience and put, them on the screen in ways that everyone can relate to. His films are entertaining—even today—because each one allows the viewer to constantly ask the question "What would I do if that were me?" Some of his best and most popular suspense films all hit the big screen in a single decade: *Stage Fright* (1950), *Strangers on a Train* (1951), *I Confess* (1953), *Dial M for Murder* (1954), *Rear Window* (1954), *The Man Who Knew Too Much* (1956), *Vertigo* (1958), *North by Northwest* (1959) and *Psycho* (1960). Study his techniques, as they will help you with your own writing.

Unlike the murder mystery, the suspense drama is primarily about *preventing* a murder or unthinkable crime. What counts most in creating suspense is the thrill of the chase.

How to Write a Contemporary Thriller

The contemporary thriller film is, more or less, an amalgamation of the murder mystery, noir and suspense drama. Much like the action-adventure genre, thrillers mix and match elements from all three to create the illusion of something new and unique for the movie-going audience. But, as they say in the film industry, there's nothing new. You can only re-invent what's been done before. That's the nature of making a thriller (or any genre) screenplay commercially appealing to agents, managers and studio executives.

In 2005, writer-director Rian Johnson—several years out of film school—paid homage to film noir in his teen crime thriller *Brick*. Johnson reinvented the genre by using classic elements such as witty dialogue and voice-over, but replacing the hard-boiled detective with a loner teenager seeking to avenge the murder of the girl he loved. Johnson admits that the works of Dashiell Hammett (*The Maltese Falcon*) originally inspired the film. He won the Special Jury Prize for Originality of Vision at the 2005 Sundance Film Festival for this effort.

Popular Thriller Film Sub-Genres

Given Hollywood's effort to re-invent the thriller, there is now a long list of sub-genres. Here are examples of the most popular:[5]

- The **science-fiction-action thriller**: the *Star Wars* franchise (1977–2005), the *X-Men* franchise (2000–2006) and *War of the Worlds* (2005). So far in the twenty-first century, this is the most popular form of thriller.

- The **action-adventure thriller**: the *James Bond* franchise (1965–2006), *Blood Diamond* (2006) and *The Departed* (2006). This genre is right up there with the sci-fi thrillers in popularity.

- The **legal thriller**: *Presumed Innocent* (1990), *The Firm* (1993) and *Runaway Jury* (2003).

- The **medical thriller**: *Outbreak* (1995).

- The **political thriller**: *The Sum of All Fears* (2002), *The Manchurian Candidate* (2004), the *Bourne* trilogy (2002–2007) and *Syriana* (2005).

- The **psychological thriller**: *The Talented Mr. Ripley* (1999), *Mystic River* (2003), *The Village* (2004) and *History of Violence* (2005).

- The **romantic relationship thriller**: *Fatal Attraction* (1987) and *Single White Female* (1992).

- The **woman/child-in-jeopardy thriller:** *Thelma & Louise* (1991), *Man on Fire* (2004), *The Interpreter* (2005) and *Flight Plan* (2005).
- The **techno thriller:** *The Net* (1995), *Minority Report* (2002) and *Firewall* (2006).
- The **horror thriller:** *Rosemary's Baby* (1968), *The Exorcist* (1973), *The Silence of the Lambs* (1991) and *The Sixth Sense* (1999).
- The **graphic novel thriller:** the *X-Men* franchise (2000–2006), *Road to Perdition* (2002), *League of Extraordinary Gentlemen* (2003), the *Fantastic Four* movies (2005, 2007), *History of Violence* (2005) and *Sin City* (2005).
- The **fantasy thriller:** the *Lord of the Rings* trilogy (2001–2003), the *Harry Potter franchise* (2001–2008) and *The Chronicles of Narnia* (2005–2008).

Hollywood's Love Affair with "Thrilling" Suspense

The film industry is obsessed with youth. And in its efforts to appeal to younger audiences, films in the thriller genre have become one of the vehicles of choice. This effort embraces the "dark side" of humanity, which is a throwback to the classic noir style in many ways. Comic-book heroes are a rich source. More and more, the superhero graphic novel is finding its way onto the big screen. To appeal to a more youthful ticket buyer, studios are casting roles in these films against type. For example, in *Road to Perdition* (2002) Tom Hanks plays an unapologetic hit man. Because of popular video games, excessive violence is at the heart of the youth movement for studios; the *Sin City* film franchise is a prime example.

Figure 3.2   *Top-Ten Grossing Domestic Box Office Thrillers of All Time*[6]

1. *The Da Vinci Code* ($217 million)
2. *The Bourne Supremacy* ($176 million)
3. *Air Force One* ($172 million)
4. *Casino Royale* ($167 million)
5. *Hannibal* ($165 million)
6. *Fatal Attraction* ($156 million)
7. *Mission: Impossible* 3 ($134 million)

8. *The Departed* ($132 million)
9. *Silence of the Lambs* ($130 million)
10. *Traffic* ($124 million)

Choose What to Write

Thrillers are always in demand. Granted, the more commercial ones are sub-genres, with action and science fiction at the top of the list. When trying to decide what type of thriller to write, one approach is to do what consumer advertising executives call a *gap analysis*: look at what hasn't been made for a while within popular sub-genres—there are websites containing past years' box office results—and write a screenplay to fill that gap.

I recommend that you work to come up with a pure mystery thriller. For years, my agent nagged me to write a screenplay like *Wait Until Dark*. This 1967 screenplay was written by Robert Carrington and Fredrick Knott, based on Knott's stage play. Here is the basic story concept:[7]

> A blind housewife becomes the target of three thugs, who are searching for the heroin hidden in a doll her husband transported from Canada as a favor to a woman who since has been murdered. The trio tries to convince the blind woman that her spouse is implicated in the crime and that the only way to protect him is to surrender the doll. More murder and mayhem ensue when she refuses. In the final scene, the blind woman levels the playing field by plunging her apartment into total darkness, and then she is able to outwit the villains.

The pure mystery thriller is always in demand, even though it does not necessarily generate high box office results. But stars like to do them, especially the aging leading men looking to create new acting opportunities. Your ultimate goal as a screenwriter is to sell a script, and if you write an intriguing, taut mystery thriller, it will become a lightning rod for your career.

Do the "Heavy Lifting"

Because of the complicated nature of thriller storytelling, it's crucial to the writing process to do your homework. The time you spend creating the various elements for your thriller will pay off in spades when you write the actual screenplay. There's nothing more terrifying than getting lost in your own mystery while you're writing it!

Thrillers & Casting

As with most popular film genres, the characters must attract recognizable actors. More and more, stars are looking for different kinds of roles to play, especially interesting villains. For example, in 2007, Kevin Costner (*Dances with Wolves* and *JFK*) played the title role villain in *Mr. Brooks*, a serial killer in a twelve-step program.

However, in the case of the thriller, studios more often than not cast the "up and coming" stars. One reason for this is that these actors are cheaper than the well-known stars. In 2006, the "up and coming" short list included Jake Gyllenhaal from the sci-fi thriller *The Day After Tomorrow* (2004) and the murder mystery thriller *Zodiac* (2007)—his quote is $5–7 million; Scarlett Johansson from the romance thriller *Match Point* and *The Island* (both 2005)—she gets $5–9 million per film; Clive Owen from the graphic novel crime thriller *Sin City* and *Derailed* (both 2005)—he earns $5 million per picture; and Rachel McAdams from the thriller *Red Eye* (2005)—her salary per movie is $3–4 million.[8]

The Most Important Dramatic Roles to Develop

As a screenwriter, consider the following three dramatic roles when you develop your cast of characters:

The handsome leading man is a role that can attract pop culture actors and generate ticket sales from the "Sexiest Man Alive" generation of young women.

The femme fatale is a role that can attract "hot" actresses, which draws young men into theaters. This character is generally portrayed (and cast) as more "experienced" in life, though age doesn't necessarily have to be a factor.

The ingénue is the role that—more and more—attracts emerging female pop singers and fashion models who have acting ambitions. This female role is portrayed (and cast) as more "naïve" in life, which implies youth.

Heavy Lifting & the Fairytales

Because The Three Little Pigs has two "murders" and an evil "serial killer," I almost chose to use it again as a template for a thriller genre script. Instead, I'm going with Little Red Riding Hood because, first and foremost, it has the strong potential to create a story around the vital central element in all good thrillers: *betrayal.*

The Most Important Roles to Cast: Heroes & Villains

I'll begin by selecting my hero, because the hero in a thriller is the character who solves the crime. In literature, they're more aptly called *sleuths.* There are several different types.[9]

The amateur. This could be anyone—even you. Using this type of sleuth has the benefit of putting the audience right in the protagonist's shoes, totally involving the audience in the solving of the crime and making the crime "personal." This keeps the sleuth's actions and reactions on a more emotional level.

The semi-pro. This protagonist has detective skills but is not actually a detective per se. These are people whose jobs involve being curious, not necessarily crime solving, such as journalists and lawyers. This type of detective also allows for more audience participation in the mystery-solving process and brings a more sophisticated level to the procedure, making it more logical than emotional. The semi-pro must strive to be objective, unlike the amateur.

The private investigator. This sleuth is trained and licensed and is equipped to protect him or herself if necessary. However, he or she is not bound by most legal restraints and professional ethics, except within the rules of keeping one's license. This type of sleuth can cross all kinds of legal lines with little or no repercussions. However, you must take care to give the P.I. a recognizable moral code so the audience will know how to feel about him or her, whether to have sympathy for him or her when straying out of bounds.

The police. The law represents society's moral standards, and cops are specially charged with maintaining order and exacting justice within the rule of the law. This type of sleuth makes it possible for the screenwriter to more closely explore morality and its relevance for the audience. It's important to pay attention to the time in which the story takes place, because morals change from generation to generation.

Choose the Protagonist & Sub-Genre

Because the essence of Little Red Riding Hood is a young girl in jeopardy, I'm developing a female-in-jeopardy story combined with the medical thriller sub-genre to give the story a viewpoint. My heroine will be a semi-pro. The mental image I'm using for her is of Natalie Portman (*Closer* [2004], *Star Wars Episode III: Revenge of the Sith* and *V for Vendetta* [both 2005]). Here's her thumbnail sketch:

> *Belinda Hood* (late twenties) dropped out of the medical field in the middle of her internship at New York Presbyterian Hospital to pursue a dream she'd pushed aside to appease the wishes of her now-estranged parents. She's the girl next door with an eye-catching head of natural red hair she inherited from her tough-minded grandmother, *Millicent Hood*, who'd always encouraged her to pursue her dream of being a photojournalist. Fearless to a fault, Belinda works at the *New York Tribune* covering the crime beat. She's garnered some notoriety with her photo essays on violence in the South Bronx. Still, she feels she has to prove herself continually to everyone (except her grandmother) and, at times, can be very annoying to those who don't want her poking around in their affairs.

Give Your Hero a Strong Goal

Like in all good screenplays, your thriller protagonist should have a strong and measurable goal in the story and plot. In keeping with the spirit of Little Red Riding Hood, Belinda has to solve the murder of her beloved grandmother, Millicent, because the police are dragging their feet on the investigation. In the process, Belinda uncovers a conspiracy and must work to put a stop to it.

Choose a Villain

The opposing side of the conflict equation involves the villain. Take the time to sketch out the physical, social and psychological profile of your villain. (For help, use Appendix C: *Thriller Worksheet*.) The more interesting the villain, the stronger potential there will be to attract a well-known actor. In thrillers, there are two basic types of villains:

The desperate average person. If the protagonist is an anti-hero (that's a villain's story), you must answer the big question for the audience: "Why can't he (or she) just call the cops?"[10]

The seemingly invincible. This brings to mind the story of David and Goliath, or your next-door neighbor going up against a superior, intelligent, often witty and sly opponent. The narrative spine of your screenplay depends on this type of relationship.

My villain is an ambitious police detective who is seemingly invincible. His name is *Jackson Wolfe* (sticking with the Little Red Riding Hood villain's name). The image of this character in my mind is that of Clive Owen of *Closer* (2004), *Sin City* (2005) and *Children of Men* (2006). He has on-screen intensity, yet also shows vulnerability, and he has great chemistry with Natalie Portman in *Closer*. I expect the image of these two flirting while bumping heads in my story will serve my muse well. Here's a thumbnail sketch:

> Detective Lieutenant *Jackson Wolfe* (thirty-ish) is obsessed with becoming the youngest Chief of Detectives in the NYPD and must hurdle several veteran captains who are currently in line for the job. He's known as the go-to guy when it comes solving the tough cases. His detractors accuse him of planting and falsifying evidence (he jokes that he'll only do that if he's sure the suspect is guilty), but no one has been able to prove these allegations. He's the quiet strong type, and when he speaks he can be intimating. But mostly he's very charming, especially when it comes to beautiful women.
>
> The *ultimate* villain—the man pulling all the strings—is *Anderson Philmore*, Chief Executive Officer of Bexis Research, Inc., a giant pharmaceutical conglomerate. He's rich and powerful—and he didn't get that way by being a nice guy.

Give Your Villain a Strong Goal

The villain is at the heart of the thriller, because this character sets the height of the bar that the hero or heroine must hurdle. Wolfe plays a key part in a conspiracy to cover up the brutal murder of Belinda's grandmother. His payoff—the appointment as NYPD's Chief of Detectives. For most of the story, he will appear to be the tough-but-duty-bound police officer determined to solve the story's murder while making passes at Belinda. This provides the opportunity to explore the requisite thriller theme of betrayal in the mainplot.

The Other Important Dramatic Roles

My twist on the femme fatale motif is an *homme fatale*: the handsome Editor in Chief and only son of the owner of the *New York Tribune* newspaper where Belinda works. He'll turn out to be a part of the same conspiracy in which Lt. Wolfe is involved. As the image for this character, I visualize actor Russell Crowe. Here's my thumbnail sketch:

> *William Morgan* (mid-forties) is urbane and intelligent. As the Editor in Chief, he's dedicated to the family business. Or so it seems. Belinda falls for William, and she falls hard. But of course, he's using her for his own end: to become wealthy and independent of the family fortune, thus stepping out of the shadow of his revered father.

My ingénue is Belinda's attractive but naïve assistant/researcher. She's French, a budding reporter and a feminist. I'm using the image of Mandy Moore (*American Dreamz*, 2006), an up-and-coming young actress. Here's my thumbnail sketch:

> *Arabelle Rouseau* (twenty-two) is a man-hater, and she cloaks her contempt for men beneath her feminist rhetoric. She's lived in New York since she was eighteen, speaks English fluently, but holds on to her French accent by choice. Her father's a high-profile diplomat (who maintains a mistress, perhaps the source of Arabelle's disdain for men) at the United Nations. Her mother, a fashion designer, chooses to live and work in Paris (and also chooses to let her husband do as he pleases; another source of resentment for Arabelle). Arabelle has a great sense of humor and is well liked.

The murder victim. In Little Red Riding Hood, the grandmother dies by getting eaten by the wolf. So shall mine. But she'll be meticulously sliced to death with a surgeon's scalpel. The image I'm using for this character is of the older (and beloved) Ann Bancroft, who unfortunately left this life in 2005. Here's a thumbnail sketch:

> *Millicent Hood* (seventy-five) is—or should I say, *was*—a very sophisticated, kind, but tough-as-nails and well-educated woman. You might even say she was a borderline feminist, having come of age in the 1950s when beautiful women were trophies. She's still a looker, too. She's always encouraged her granddaughter, Belinda, to pursue her dreams, which flew in the face of her own daughter's wishes for Belinda. When

Belinda announced that she was quitting her medical internship, Millicent's daughter stopped talking to her.

Key suspects. It's important to your story to have the audience actively participate in the in-progress plot. Challenge your protagonist with a list of suspects to eliminate. For now, I'm starting with three. Perhaps a few more will need development as I progress in the expansion of the basic story and plot, but three is a magic number that always works in storytelling (and comedy; see Chapter 6 for more on this).

The *red herrings* are *Dr. Frank Scott*, Millicent's surgeon, who is accused of murdering her, and . . .

Dr. Ivan Jankovich, a Serbian scientist who specializes in the human genome (DNA), and . . .

Of course, *Anderson Philmore*, who starts out as a pivotal character and will evolve to become a co-villain.

Develop Your Thriller Premise

To be perfectly clear, let's start with the definition of a thriller:

> *A story in which the protagonist gets caught up in a web of danger, intrigue and deception and must use "brains over brawn" to defeat an individual or group of powerful opponents.*[11]

You must create a high-concept premise that revolves around the "web of danger." (See the section in Chapter 1 on creating an enticing film premise.) It's that simple. Here are some examples from films:

Syriana (2005) revolves about the web of danger of a CIA agent caught between his job with the CIA covert operations involving a potential terrorist attack and the State Department's investigation of a big oil company's Middle Eastern operations.

The Interpreter (2005) revolves around the web of danger of an interpreter caught between her country's loyalties and the U.S. Secret Service when she overhears a plot to murder her country's leader while he addresses the United Nations.

A History of Violence (2005) revolves around the web of danger of a mild-mannered, well-respected diner owner in a small town caught between being a hero after thwarting an armed robbery and the mobsters who show up claiming he's a hit man running away from his past.

The stories that evolve from these webs of danger are especially sophisticated, as are most premises for the thriller genre. However, each one effectively puts the protagonist between a rock and hard place, where their past and present lives collide.

Here's the basic premise for the fairytale Little Red Riding Hood:

> When going to visit her sick grandmother, Little Red Riding Hood confides in a charismatic wolf who betrays her by eating her grandmother and, in the end, eats Little Red Riding Hood as well.

My web of danger finds my heroine, Belinda Hood, caught between the NYPD and a multinational pharmaceutical conglomerate. Here's a contemporary high-concept thriller premise from this fairytale:

> *After a photojournalist's grandmother is ritualistically murdered with a surgeon's scalpel, she sets out to find the killer but finds herself caught between the NYPD and a multinational pharmaceutical conglomerate—both hellbent on preventing the revelation of the truth*

I set my story in New York City, a jungle of sorts, as a metaphor for the "woods" in the fairytale. There'll be key scenes in my screenplay that take place in the woods to further utilize this metaphor.

Create an Intriguing Thriller Title

It helps for your title to be clever and, ideally, you should come up with a double entendre: a word or phrase having two meanings, especially if one is sexually suggestive. You'll generally find this to be true with successful thrillers. The right title of a thriller, like an action-adventure, can encourage it to be read, and the title is also critical to the marketing of the finished film. In large part, the term *fatal attraction* is a mainstay in American dating vernacular because of the film of the same name. But the thriller *Fatal Attraction* (1987) didn't start out with that title; its working title was *Diversions* (based on the title of the short film that inspired the feature film). Would *Casablanca* have exuded the same aura of intrigue and romance if it had released under its original title, *Everybody Comes to Rick's?*[12]

My working title for Little Red Riding Hood is *Cutline*, which refers to the caption under a newspaper photograph. Since my heroine is a photojournalist, I thought this would be highly appropriate. "Cut" is a key syllable, since the murderer uses a surgeon's scalpel. This makes the title a double entendre.

Choose Your Thriller Theme

It's imperative to grapple with the concept of morality when developing your thriller. You must deal with the concepts of right and wrong (good versus evil). While this is the primary theme of thriller films, you can also narrow the focus to something more specific for your particular story and the characters involved. A surefire technique is to go to the table of contents in *Roget's International Thesaurus* and look under the class of words called "Affections" and subtitled "Morality." There you will find a substantial list of more specific words on which you can base your general theme of good versus evil. You could take the word "justice" and base your screenplay on it as the one-word theme, then work from there to both the physical and metaphysical central questions. (See the section in Chapter 1 on story theme.)

But don't forget, in the thriller genre, the protagonist is almost always walking a thin line between good and evil, or at the very least is struggling with whether to do things in a way that's morally right or morally wrong. As is often true in life, the right way is not always the best way. Then there's the human tendency to seek revenge, which swirls through nearly every entertaining thriller story.

The moral of the fairytale Little Red Riding Hood could be summed up as "don't talk to strangers" or "beware of strangers." My theme revolves around trust and betrayal. Like in the fairytale, Belinda trusts the police—represented by Jackson Wolfe—but she learns that he does not have her best interest at heart as she tries to find her grandmother's killer.

Morality's Point of View: Exception to the Rule

The anti-hero (or anti-heroine) is essentially a study of evil. This is a simple reversal of a story's point of view. Instead of the audience following the hero, they follow the villain—from his or her point of view. The thriller genre is ideal for this approach. Examples of anti-hero thrillers are *The Usual Suspects* (1995), *The Talented Mr. Ripley* (1999) and *History of Violence* (2005)—which all tell their stories from the criminal's point of view. The hero is still an important ingredient to the anti-hero story's conflict, though, as the audience needs someone to root for, someone to stop the villain's dastardly deeds; this is also important for creating conflict. Sometimes the villain actually reforms and is redeemed in the audience's eyes because of his experiences in the story's plot, though usually by making the ultimate sacrifice and dying, such as the character Creasy (Denzel Washington) in the film *Man on Fire*.

Develop Your Thriller Story & Plot

Essentially, thrillers focus on either solving a crime or preventing a crime. The stories and plots tend to be complex. Thus, thriller story-telling ideally embraces the following key elements:

Present the hero with a series of dilemmas. Ideally, these dilemmas are moral ones—the protagonist grappling with right and wrong while trying to solve or prevent a crime.

Use a McGuffin.[13] This dramatic device keeps the plot moving forward. Most times it's an object of value—whether actual or perceived—that everyone in the story wants badly. It could also be a person that everyone wants badly, be it for love, sex or revenge.

Be unpredictable. The worst thing that can happen in a thriller is for the audience to figure out what's going to happen next. Even if the end of the story is relatively apparent—which it shouldn't be—the ride to the end should be a series of surprise plot twists and turns. The goal is to get the audience involved in the process of solving the mystery or crime.

Foster a sense of urgency. Create time pressure for the solving or prevention of a crime. Accomplish this by clearly setting a series of deadlines for the protagonist to achieve, which will have negative consequences if not met. Sometimes the villain has control over these deadlines, which can ramp up the pressure in a story.

Constantly raise the stakes. Keep upping the ante for what the protagonist has to lose by failing. That means the protagonist must first make progress in solving the crime or mystery. The way to define the stakes is to ask a simple question of your plot: what will happen if the protagonist (or villain) does not achieve his or her next objective? When the protagonist does achieve an objective in the plot, it automatically gives him or her more to lose.

Create suspense. It's necessary to get (and keep) the audience on the edge of their theater seats while watching your movie. But don't forget that your first audience is a reader (story analyst, producer, director, actor, studio executive), so you must make them keep turning the page by creating tension in the plot. Often, in an attempt to create suspense, an inexperienced writer withholds information from the reader. You must not make this mistake.

Key Elements of the Thriller

A Simple Formula: How to Create Suspense

Here's the solution, just follow this process:

What the audience and the character(s) know . . . Start on equal ground so the audience shares the same information as the character(s). This helps the audience participate in the storytelling.

What only the audience knows . . . Then it's effective to give the audience information—not all of it, but just enough to spark interest or give them a superior position—so they become anxious about what the protagonist will do without knowing what they, the audience, knows.

What only the character(s) know . . . Then let the protagonist get ahead of the audience, exacerbating the tension because now the audience doesn't know what's going to happen next and must guess.

You can swap the second and third steps in this process to create a different feeling of suspense:

The audience and the character(s) know the same thing.

The character(s) know more than the audience.

The audience knows more than the characters.

To illustrate this technique, here's a simple scene example.

A woman steps into a dark hallway and tries to turn on the lights, but they don't work. She stares down the dark hall, takes a breath and starts walking. (*This in itself is not suspenseful, but certainly portends of danger.*)

Around the corner, the audience sees a man waiting, who pulls out a knife when he hears the sound of footsteps. (*Now there is a palatable sense of anticipation as the woman moves closer to the turn in the hallway. The audience knows more than the character.*)

Just as the woman nears the turn in the hallway, she stops because she's forgotten something. (*We hold our breath as the man must decide whether to peek around the corner to see what's going on or attack now.*)

The woman turns around and walks back the way she came. (*Now the audience wonders what the man will do; more tension.*)

The woman stops again, decides she doesn't need what she left behind, and starts back toward the corner of the hall. Now, as the footsteps get closer again, the man prepares again for the attack. The woman turns the corner but the audience doesn't see what happens—only hears the scuffle, the woman's screams and the man's grunts. (*Now the character has more information than the audience does, so the audience must wait in anticipation of the outcome.*)

Finally the woman emerges—covered in blood, holding the knife—and the man falls dead. (*The audience and the character are back on equal ground, relieving the tension.*)

Use this same approach with a series of scenes to form a very suspenseful sequence in the story and plot. You can also apply this formula to the entire story and plot.

Use Thriller Hallmarks

The thriller screenplay utilizes these vital techniques.

Use cliffhangers. Write scenes whose outcome is uncertain. The idea is to pull the audience to the edge of their collective seats by not giving a scene an ending, only a beginning and middle. Make the audience wait a few scenes or, when appropriate, make them wait until the end of the story before revealing the truth.

Exploit secrets. The thriller thrives on secrets—secrets kept from both the protagonist and the audience. So the protagonist should have a secret or two that are not immediately shared with the audience and are only hinted at as the story unfolds, before being fully revealed at an auspicious time.

Invent twists and turns. The goal is to prevent the audience from knowing what's going to happen next. You want them guessing—but not guessing correctly. Part and parcel to this technique is using the audience's own knowledge and sophistication against them. You can achieve this by leading the audience down what appears to be a predictable path, then turning the tables on them.

Create a red herring. This term comes from the fact that red herring do not exist in nature but are created during the preparation process. The red herring character *looks* guilty, but is proven innocent at some point.

Develop a list of suspects. There must always be a list of potentially guilty people. This list is what the sleuth must wade through in order to solve or prevent the crime. Make this a game with which the audience can play along.

Plant hidden clues. As the first half of the thriller unfolds, it's important to hide clues from the protagonist in order to create suspense. Part of this technique, as mentioned earlier, is sharing bits of these clues with the audience so they can anticipate when and how the protagonist will discover them more fully.

Put clues in plain sight. There should be some clues that seem like something else along the way for both the protagonist and the audience to discover. These clues become apparent once only enough information comes to light.

Develop the Thriller's Dual Plot Structure

The thriller genre uses a two story/plot approach. The *apparent plot* is what the audience *thinks* is happening, but the *real plot* is what is *really* happening.

The thriller story/plot begins with either a crime being committed (the mystery) or the plan to commit a crime (the suspense drama). The protagonist begins moving in one direction (the apparent plot) while the villain executes his scheme (the real plot). As the apparent plot unfolds, the protagonist comes across clues that are not obvious to him or her or the audience. As the protagonist progresses, he or she gets more and more involved in the villain's scheme and even sometimes becomes an unwitting pawn. Sooner or later—generally at the plot's midpoint—the protagonist realizes what's going on and turns the tables on the villain by using brains over brawn.

While not all the details of the villain's conspiracy are clear to the protagonist or the audience, the thrill ride has two sides to it: (1) the solving or prevention of the crime and (2) the big surprises in the process. It's important to plant clues in the first half of the plot—called *foreshadowing* or *set-ups*—and have them gradually make sense in the second half of the plot—the *pay-offs*.

It's this double storytelling that makes the thriller a challenging genre to write well.

Figure 3.1   *Thriller Story/Plot Structure*

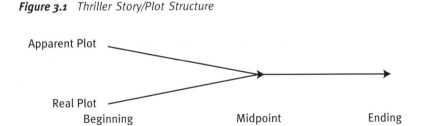

Cutline: The Apparent Plot

The story opens with *Belinda Hood* going to visit her sick grandmother, *Millicent Hood*, at her Montauk, Long Island manor. Belinda finds her grandmother dead, murdered in a ritualistic manner. She recognizes the murder weapon as a surgeon's scalpel. She meets Detective Lieutenant *Jackson Wolfe* when he's assigned to the murder case. He assures Belinda that they will find and prosecute the murderer. Millicent's doctor, *Frank Scott*, is the prime suspect. But Belinda soon realizes that the NYPD is dragging its feet on the investigation, so she sets out to uncover evidence on her own. She has the help of her assistant researcher, *Arabelle Rouseau*.

The investigation leads Belinda to Bexis Research, Inc., a giant pharmaceutical conglomerate that's about to launch a new miracle drug, HIX-10, which has been approved by the FDA to treat HIV/AIDS. When Belinda begins to uncover shady activities in the company's past, Bexis' CEO, *Anderson Philmore,* puts pressure on Lt. Wolfe to get control of Belinda—she's threatening their product introduction. But Belinda is not so easily discouraged.

Dr. Ivan Jankovich, a Serbian scientist and DNA expert who's working on the drug development, dies in a car accident. Belinda discovers that Ivan's death was not an accident but a murder to cover up data showing the true results of HIX-10's medical trials. She also learns that her grandmother had stumbled upon the truth—quite by mistake—and that's what got her killed.

Belinda's life is in grave danger when she discovers the core of the conspiracy: a fake viral strain that will distract from HIX-10's side effects of permanent blindness and deafness in patients. Dr. Scott is ready to go public with what he knows, but then he's brutally murdered.

When she learns that Philmore has promised Lt. Jackson Wolfe his dream job—Chief of Detectives at the NYPD—Belinda realizes who the real murderer is. Now she is in a race against time to find the digital flash drive containing the proof before it's destroyed or before she's killed. When she tries to reveal the truth publicly, she learns that her boss and secret lover, William Morgan, stands to earn millions of dollars from stock options of HIX-10. Now she knows he's betrayed her all along. In the end, she outsmarts both Wolfe and Morgan—who she ends up killing in self-defense—and lives to see Philmore arrested for his crimes.

Cutline: The Real Plot (The Villain's Conspiracy)

A new drug, HIX-10, which has been developed to treat HIV/AIDS, appears to work extremely well. But in reality, the drug's side effects leave many patients irreversibly blind and deaf. To prevent the lost of billions of dollars in global sales, Bexis Research, Inc., falsifies the drug trials. And to ensure avoiding law suits in the long term, the company devises a way to make the side effects appear to be a new viral strain of HIV/AIDS, thus ensuring that the company will make huge profits for years to come. The kicker: they plan to miraculously come up with the cure for the new HIV strain they've invented and make billions more.

There's one final touch: the McGuffin, a digital flash drive containing damaging drug-trial test data and the procedure to fake the new viral strain.

The plot—the events created by the characters' actions—will be carefully worked out from these dual stories, and I will invent twists and turns along the way.

The Love Story Subplot

The last thing you need to develop is the thriller's *emotional core*—a love story that will make the audience care about your protagonist as well as the story's outcome. I will tell my emotional story by weaving it through the murder-mystery plot. Here's the love story subplot for *Cutline*.

Belinda Hood has a crush on her boss, *William Morgan* (the homme fatale). Her research assistant, *Arabelle Rouseau* (the ingénue), is a man-hater who covers her contempt for men with her feminist ideals. When Arabelle catches Belinda flirting with the boss, she resents it intensely and eventually confronts Belinda. Belinda tries to convince Arabelle that she's only using her feminine wiles to get ahead at the newspaper, but the reality is that she's fallen hard for Morgan. Even when Belinda finds out that William will profit from the conspiracy to cover up the side effects of HIX-10, she can't end their intense relationship. The last straw for Belinda is learning that William actually gave the order to kill Millicent and has been using Belinda's emotional obsession to his advantage in order to get HIX-10 to the global marketplace and make millions of dollars of his own.

In the end, Belinda lets her lust for revenge get the best of her, and she kills William in a self-defensive emotional rage when she learns that he's essentially her grandmother's murderer. Arabelle learns a lesson about love and obsession, while Belinda realizes that using one's feminine wiles is tricky business when it comes to career advancement.

Create a Blueprint

Now combine all the elements you've developed into an expanded story treatment. (See a sample in Chapter 4: Science-Fiction-Fantasy.)

Use the Thriller Writing Style

Many of the writing style techniques discussed in the action-adventure chapter also apply here: use the white space of the page, write visually, avoid camera language, use active verbs and write tight all also apply to thriller writing. Like other genres, it's important for the style of writing in your thriller screenplay to create an intriguing tone and atmosphere. Use language in action descriptions that creates noir-ish visual images. For an example, think of the style used in the novel *The Maltese Falcon* by Dashiell Hammett (1894–1961); the film version received three Oscar nominations, including Best Screenplay, adapted by venerable writer-director John Huston. This style is associated with the thriller and is an excellent one to imitate. Here's an excerpt from the novel to give you a sense of the tone. You're writing a screenplay where visual images are paramount and, though this is a novel, it achieves that end especially well.

> The *tappity-tap-tap* and the thin bell and muffled whir of Effie Perine's typewriting came through the closed door. Somewhere in a neighboring office a power-driven machine vibrated dully. On Spade's desk a limp cigarette smoldered in a brass tray filled with the remains of limp cigarettes. Ragged grey flakes of cigarette-ash dotted the yellow top of the desk and the green blotter and the papers that were there. A buff-curtained window, eight or ten inches open, let in from the court a current of air faintly scented with ammonia. The ashes on the desk twitched and crawled in the current.[14]

By the way, if you haven't already guessed it, the statuette that everyone is looking for in the *Maltese Falcon* is the McGuffin.

Here's an exchange between the heroine and villain from my spec screenplay *One Dead Slob, Two Village Idiots & Three Soul Brothers*. I've combined the use of witty voice-over, dialogue, intrigue and secrecy. Also note that I'm using darkness and shadows to create a mysterious atmosphere.

```
INT. COLLEGE CHANCELLOR'S OFFICE - NIGHT
```

Dark. Quiet. Until the light from a goose-neck desk lamp snaps on, spilling a pool of light over the rich oak desk.

It's Angela.

> ANGELA (V.O.)
> So, I went to search Father's desk
> for clues . . .

In a hurry, she searches the drawers. At the final drawer, her eye catches something. She takes a vial of prescription pills, puts it under the lamp to read the label:

"Phenothazine" and the name "Eugene Brown."

> ANGELA (V.O.)
> It was Phenothazine . . .

> ANGELA
> What the hell is Phenothazine?

A photo on the wall catches her eye as she pockets the empty vial. She cranks the goose-neck lamp to take a closer look at it:

Dan Burkhardt posing with Cliff "The Man" Morgan and the Mayor of Bartlett.

> ANGELA
> Big fat jock sniffer.

Angela renews her search, this time finds a:

Nickel-plated snub-nose .38 Special.

> ROSE (O.S.)
> Burkhardt's little toy, no doubt . . .

Angela nearly jumps out of her skin, turns to see:

Rose filling the doorway, backlit from the light in the hallway.

> ROSE
> What are you doing rifling through a
> dead man's desk?

```
                    ANGELA
          It was Father's desk, too. If only
          for a few days.

                    ANGELA (V.O.)
          I resented her tone of voice . . .

                    ROSE
          Is that resentment I hear?

                    ANGELA
          He forgot something.

                    ROSE
          You're right. His spine. I'll take
          care of this.

     Rose takes the revolver from Angela, slips it
     inside her black leather handbag.

                    ROSE
          Did you find what you were looking for?

                    ANGELA
          No. It wasn't here.
          (beat)
          Why are you here so late?

     Rose looks right into Angela's eyes:

                    ROSE
          Tell your gutless father that everything
          in this office is going. Everything.

     Rose flicks off the goose-neck lamp, leaving only
     the light from the open door slashing inside.

                    ROSE (SUGARY)
          Are you coming, darling?

     Angela follows her mother out.

                    ANGELA (V.O.)
          Now I was convinced Mother was some-
          how involved in this mess.
```

Thriller Writing Examples from Produced Screenplays

Here are some examples of action descriptions written by top screenwriters.

M. Night Shyamalan thrills the reader in his horror-thriller screenplay *The Sixth Sense* (1999):

The girl reaches out with her withered and emaci-
ated hands—tiny tubes hang from her wrists. She
scratches Cole as he tumbles back, terrified, out
of the tent. The whole tent collapses.

Brian Helgeland creates a exhilarating car chase in the screenplay for
the political thriller *The Bourne Supremacy* (2004), based on the Robert
Ludlum novel:

MARIE at the wheel—adrenaline pumping—clear running
for thirty yards ahead and—

MARIE skidding them into the right turn—clipping
another vehicle—MIRROR SHATTERING—speeding up.

BOURNE scanning behind them—MARIE moving out to
pass—veering back! An ONCOMING BUS—just in time
and-

Quentin Tarantino and Roger Avary create the tone from classic film
noir in the screenplay *Pulp Fiction* (1994):

Her hand goes in his pocket and pulls out his
tobacco pouch. Like a little girl playing cowboy,
she spreads the tobacco on some rolling paper.
Imitating what he did earlier, licks the paper and
rolls it into a pretty good cigarette. Maybe a little too fat, but not bad for a first try. Mia
thinks so anyway. Her hand reaches back in the
pocket and pulls out his Zippo lighter. She SLAPS
the lighter against her leg, trying to light it
fancy-style like Vince did. What do you know, she
did it! Mia's one happy clam. She triumphantly
brings the fat flame up to her fat smoke, lighting
it up, then LOUDLY SNAPS the Zippo closed.

Figure 3.3 *Writers Guild of America's Greatest Thriller Screenplays*[15]

- *Casablanca* (screenplay by Julius J. and Phillip G. Epstein and Howard
  Koch. Based on the play "Everybody Comes to Rick's" by Murray Burnett
  and Joan Alison)
- *Chinatown* (written by Robert Towne)
- *Sunset Blvd.* (written by Charles Brackett, Billy Wilder and D.M.
  Marshman, Jr.)

- *Pulp Fiction* (written by Quentin Tarantino; stories by Quentin Tarantino and Roger Avary)
- *North by Northwest* (written by Earnest Lehman)
- *Double Indemnity* (screenplay by Billy Wilder and Raymond Chandler; based on the novel by James M. Cain)
- *Fargo* (written by Joel and Ethan Coen)
- *The Third Man* (screenplay and story by Graham Greene; based on the short story by Graham Greene)
- *The Sweet Smell of Success* (screenplay by Clifford Odets and Ernest Lehman; from a novelette by Ernest Lehman)
- *The Usual Suspects* (written by Christopher McQuarrie)
- *Taxi Driver* (written by Paul Schrader)
- *The Treasure of the Sierra Madre* (screenplay by John Huston; based on the novel by B. Traven)
- *The Maltese Falcon* (screenplay by John Huston; based on the novel by Dashiell Hammett)
- *The Sixth Sense* (written by M. Night Shyamalan)
- *All the President's Men* (screenplay by William Goldman; based on the book by Carl Bernstein and Bob Woodward)
- *L.A. Confidential* (screenplay by Brian Helgeland and Curtis Hanson; based on the novel by James Ellroy)
- *Silence of the Lambs* (screenplay by Ted Tally; based on the novel by Thomas Harris)
- *E.T.: The Extra-terrestrial* (written by Melissa Mathison)
- *Dog Day Afternoon* (screenplay by Frank Pierson; based on a magazine article by P.F. Kluge and Thomas Moore)
- *Rear Window* (screenplay by John Michael Hayes; based on the short story by Cornell Woolrich)
- *Psycho* (screenplay by Joseph Stefano; based on the novel by Robert Bloch)
- *Memento* (screenplay by Christopher Nolan; based on the short story "Memento Mori" by Jonathan Nolan)
- *Notorious* (written by Ben Hecht)

The Thriller & Television Series

The thriller is a staple of television programming for one simple reason: the threat of life and death is constant for the characters who appear from week to week. But because the TV audience, deep down inside, knows that the characters who appear from week to week are not really likely to die, they enjoy participating in solving the cases; often family members even compete with one another to try to figure out "whodunit." More and more, series writers kill off regular characters, effectively upping the thrill factor. So the key to a thriller television series is not so much the subject matter as the approach to the storytelling. And the heroes continually reinforce American moral values of truth and justice.

Thrillers on TV

Here is a decade-by-decade look at the thriller genre on television.[16]

The anthology was a popular approach to television series in its first decade with *Alfred Hitchcock Presents* (1955–1962), *Mike Hammer* (1956–1959)—based on the Mickey Spillane novels—and *The Twilight Zone* (1959–1964). The heroes on television in this decade were "real" heroes, ones whom the home audience could admire because of their courage and ability to walk a fine line between right and wrong.

In the 1960s, Hitchcock continued his presence on the airways with *The Alfred Hitchcock Hour* (1962–1965). *The Fugitive* (1963–1967, remade in 2000–2001) was perhaps the first "water cooler" series, causing viewers to gather around their office water coolers to discuss, on the air. Then there was *The Man from U.N.C.L.E.* (1964–1968) and *It Takes a Thief* (1968–1970) to carry on the thriller tradition.

McCloud (1970–1977) and the long running *Hart to Hart* (1979–1984)—the exploits of a crime solving husband and wife—dominated television in the early 1980s. One important element to this series' success was its romantic-comedy quality.

In the 1980s, the thriller became very popular with television viewers, spawning big viewer numbers for *Magnum, P.I.* (1980–1988), *The Hitchhiker* (1983–1991) and the MTV-generation film noir *Miami Vice* (1984–1989). A touch of ironic comedy gave the thriller in the hit series *Murder, She Wrote* (1984–1996) its own uniqueness. *Alfred Hitchcock Presents* (1985–1989) continued to showcase the master of suspense.

And to round out the decade, there was *Midnight Caller* (1988-1991). The 1980s saw thriller series take on a darker, more cynical quality than ever before.

The 1990s started with the quirky thriller series *Twin Peaks* (1990–1991). Then along came *Diagnosis Murder* (1993–2001), which used a touch of ironic comedy in its storytelling (a male version of *Murder, She Wrote*). Then there was *The Pretender* (1996–2000), *Profiler* (1996–2000)—a precursor to the popular *CSI* franchise—*Dark Skies* (1996–1997) and *La Femme Nikita* (1997–2001).

At the start of the twenty-first century, television spawned a large number of whodunit series, such as the *CSI* franchise (three of 'em), *NCIS*, the *Law & Order* franchise (four of 'em), the very gritty *The Shield*, *Damages*, *Thief*, *Cold Case*, *Veronica Mars* for the teen crowd, *Criminal Minds*, *Without a Trace*, *Numbers*, *Lost* and the action-packed political-military spy-thrillers *The Unit* and *Burn Notice*.

If you're interested in writing for television, watch it and learn about the particular series for which you plan to write your "spec."

Your Assignment

I know your brain feels like a sieve with all the little holes blocked. You'll get over it. You gotta. The thing is, you *need* to write this thriller. It's your *destiny*. You can't escape it. Your bank account depends on it.

I remember the first time I put my derrière in the chair in front of the computer. I started with the heavy lifting. It hurt all right, like a sharp needle in the eye. My palms were all sweaty. But I got over it. It wasn't easy, but I had to. So I started with the crime basics. I decided on a sub-genre. Once I did that, I was able to catch more shut-eye at night. Then I asked myself: who's my hero? And what about my villain? And I gotta have a femme fatale. I couldn't forget the ingénue either—this character has to be easy on the audience's eyes, a good casting bet. Yeah, I knew I had to keep the audience guessing. So I developed a list of suspects. Now that sucked a lot of energy outta the old noggin, and I didn't forget the red herring either. The rest started to come easily—it all fell in line like a row of ducks waddling down to the lake for swim. The high-concept premise, the good-versus-evil theme, the McGuffin, and I didn't forget to develop that dual plot. Oh yeah, there were lots of twists and turns. Then, to tug at the audience's heartstrings, I threw in a good love story, like a French chef seasoning a pot of bouillabaisse.

Yeah. Those were the days. Now it's your turn to thrill 'em. Go ahead. You can do it.

Notes

-- -◆- -- -- -- -- -- ➤

1. *One Dead Slob, Two Village Idiots & Three Soul Brothers* placed seventh in the 1999 Writers Digest writing competition.

2. Simon Wood, "Thrill Me," *Writer's Digest*, February 2006, 32.

3. Lee Horsley, "The Development of Post-war Literary and Cinematic Noir," *www.crimeculture.com/Contents/Film%20Noir.html* (accessed February 2, 2006).

4 Alain Silver and James Ursini (eds.), *Film Noir Reader 2* (Pompton Plains, NJ: Limelight Editions, 1999).

5. T. Macdonald Skilman, *Writing the Thriller* (Cincinnati, OH: Writer's Digest Books, 2000), 7–8.

6. Source: *www.boxofficemojo.com* (accessed June 5, 2007). Box office gross figures limited to the release year of each film, not cumulative to date.

7. Source: http://en.wikipedia.org/wiki/Wait_Until_Dark (accessed June 7, 2007).

8. Christine Spines, "Are They Worth It?" *Entertainment Weekly*, May 12, 2006, 31–36.

9. Gillian Roberts, *You Can Write a Mystery* (Cincinnati, OH: Writer's Digest Books, 1999), 12–15.

10. John Hill, "Writing a Thriller? Be Crazy Like a Fox," *Scr(i)pt* magazine, March/April 2004, 64.

11. Ray Morton, "Conventional Clichés—Part Three," *Scr(i)pt* magazine, March/April 2004, 76.

12. Stephen Galloway, "Working Title," *Fade In* magazine, vol. X, no. 1, 59, 66.

13. The name "McGuffin" originates from a mythical "apparatus for trapping lions in the Scottish Highlands." Hollywood legend has it that Alfred Hitchcock was stuck developing a story for one of his films. His friend,

screenwriter Angus MacPhail, suggested that Hitchcock use an object of interest in the plot. Hitchcock used uranium-ore hidden in a wine bottle in the film *Notorious* as a McGuffin. Hitchcock repeated using the device in many of his films. The McGuffin device is a staple of the thriller and often, in present-day films, is a real object important to the solving of the story's mystery.

14. You can find the rest of this excerpt from *The Maltese Falcon* at *www.reading-groupguides.com*.

15. Source: The Writers Guild of America, West, "The 101 Greatest Screenplays." The list can be found at *www.wga.org*.

16. Source: *www.tv.com*.

4

The Science-Fiction-Fantasy Genre

The Illusion of Reality

```
FADE IN:

An endless star field . . . tranquil . . . then—

WHOOSH! A fleeting glimpse of something huge
screams past—

Rocketing directly for a distant cerulean and green
sphere regally revolving in the distance—

It's a gargantuan spaceship on course for—

Earth . . .

EXT. CLEARING - CANADIAN FOREST - NIGHT

The fireball streaks across the black velvet night—

Atmospheric flames burning hot . . .

The spaceship is out of control!

Skips across the tree tops, then—

Smashes through the verdant foliage, opening up an
ugly gash in the forest . . .

Trees fall! Dust! Smoke! The ear-splitting roar of
timber cracking! Then finally stops.

Surrounded by nothing but trees, the spaceship sits
there.

SUPEROVER: "SOMEWHERE IN CANADA. 1944."

The debris, dust and smoke settle, returning still-
ness to nature . . .
```

> The scratching of crickets and the burping of
> frogs is the only "welcome wagon" for this strange
> vehicle . . .
>
>   MOLLIE (V.O.)
>   Okay, I want this cum-sucker healthy
>   enough for questioning . . .
>
>   CUT TO:
>
> INT. HALLWAY - SLEAZY MOTEL - SEATTLE WHARF - NIGHT
>
> Dark. Then the face of—
>
> MOLLIE STRYKER (30), highlighted by a lone light
> bulb. She's a handsome woman with soft, caring eyes
> and the demeanor of a pit bull. Right now she's very
> tense, wearing a Kevlar vest marked "Seattle P.D.
>
> SUPEROVER: "SEATTLE, WASHINGTON. PRESENT DAY."
>
> Moving with her are other Cops, all wearing bullet-
> proof vests.

These opening scenes set the stage for a story about missing children and aliens in one of my "spec" sci-fi screenplays. I developed this script based on a fairytale, which I will discuss later in the chapter. But first, let's take a brief stroll through the history of the science-fiction-fantasy genre.

Origins of Science-Fiction-Fantasy

It's impossible to explore this genre without recognizing the influence of novelists Jules Verne (1828–1905), who wrote *Journey to the Center of the Earth*, and H.G. Wells (1866–1946), who penned an array of fine science-fiction novels, including *The Time Machine* in 1895, *The Invisible Man* in 1897, *The War of the Worlds* in 1898 and *The First Men in the Moon* in 1901, all of which spawned film versions. Another influential novelist is Ray Bradbury (b. 1920), who wrote *The Martian Chronicles* in 1950 and *Fahrenheit 451* in 1953. Bradbury also wrote the original story for the science-fiction film *It Came from Outer Space* (1953). During 2001–2003, *The Lord of the Rings* fantasy novels by J.R.R. Tolkien (1892–1973) were developed into a trilogy of films, becoming among the top box office film successes of all time. Now the series of seven novels written by C.S. Lewis (1898–1963)—*The Chronicles of Narnia*—are being portrayed on the silver screen.

It's important as a screenwriter to understand the definition of the science-fiction genre:

> *Films that deal with the effects of change on people in the real world as it can be projected into the past, the future or to distant places. This genre often concerns itself with scientific or technological change, and it usually involves matters whose importance is greater than the individual or the community; often civilization or the race itself is in danger.*[1]

Figure 4.1 *Types of Science-Fiction-Fantasy Stories*[2]

- Far Travel
- The Wonders of Science
- Man & Machine
- Progress
- Man & Society
- Man in the Future
- War
- Cataclysm
- Man & Environment
- Superpowers
- Superman
- Man & Alien
- Man & Religion
- Glimpses into the Past and Future

Fiction that depicts innovations ruled out by current scientific theory, such as stories about faster-than-light travel, may be classified as science fiction. For this reason, the line between fantasy and science fiction is blurred; many bookstores shelve science fiction and fantasy together. There's a substantial overlap between the audiences of science fiction and fantasy literature, and many science-fiction authors have also written works of fantasy (and vice versa).[3]

Precursors to the contemporary genre—such as Mary Shelley's gothic novel *Frankenstein, or the Modern Prometheus* (1818), the same author's post-apocalyptic *The Last Man* (1826) and Robert Louis Stevenson's *The Strange Case of Dr. Jekyll and Mr. Hyde* (1886)—are plainly science fiction, whereas Bram Stoker's *Dracula* (1897), which is based on the supernatural, is not. A borderline case is Mark Twain's *A Connecticut Yankee in King Arthur's Court* (1889), where the time travel is unexplained, but subsequent events make realistic use of science. Shelley's novel and Stevenson's novella are early examples of a standard science-fiction theme: the obsessed scientist whose discoveries worsen a bad circumstance.[4]

Early in the history of silent film, the science-fiction film established a genre of its own, generally more sensational and less scientific than literature. One of the first important science-fiction films was Fritz Lang's *Metropolis* (1927). After a dry period during the war years (World War II and the Korean War), science-fiction films rose in popularity during what has been dubbed the "golden age" of science-fiction films. Despite this exalted title, many of the 1950s sci-fi flicks had corny dialogue, poor screenplays, bad acting and amateurish production values. In response to a growing interest in rocketry and space exploration, feature-length space-travel films gained popularity in the early 1950s, pioneered by two 1950 films: *Rocketship X-M* and *Destination Moon*.[5]

Figure 4.2   *Classic Low-Budget Sci-Fi Films*[6]

- *Flight to Mars* (1951)
- *The Thing from Another World* (1951)
- *The Day the Earth Stood Still* (1951)
- *When Worlds Collide* (1951)
- *It Came from Outer Space* (1953)
- *Invaders from Mars* (1953)
- *The War of the Worlds* (1953)
- *Them!* (1954)
- *Creature from the Black Lagoon* (1954)
- *This Island Earth* (1955)
- *Conquest of Space* (1955)

- *Earth vs. the Flying Saucers* (1956)
- *It Conquered the World* (1956)
- *Invasion of the Body Snatchers* (1956)
- *Not of This Earth* (1957)
- *Attack of the Crab Monsters* (1957)
- *The Incredible Shrinking Man* (1957)
- *I Married a Monster from Outer Space* (1958)

It has often been said that science-fiction film lags about fifty years behind science-fiction literature, with a film such as *Star Wars* (1977) resembling the pulp science fiction in *Planet Stories*[6] as an excellent example. After *Star Wars* hit the big screen, almost every year since there has been at least one sciene-fiction blockbuster.[7]

Popular Science-Fiction-Fantasy Sub-Genres

In the categories below, note that many science-fiction-fantasy films include significant elements of the action-adventure genre.

Alien invasion: *War of the Worlds* (1953, remade in 2005), *Independence Day (1996) and Transformers* (2007).

Creatures and monsters: the *Alien* franchise (1979–1997), the Jurassic Park franchise (1993–2001), *I, Robot* (2004), *King Kong* (2005) and *I Am Legend* (2007).

Time travel: the *Star Trek* franchise (1979–2002), the *Terminator* franchise (1984–2003), *Twelve Monkeys* (1995) and *Frequency* (2000).

Action-adventure-thriller: the *Planet of the Apes* franchise (1968–2001), the *Star Wars* franchise (1977–2005), the *Batman* franchise (1989–2005) and *The Matrix* trilogy (1999–2003).

Fantasy: the *Superman* franchise (1978–2006), the *Lord of the Rings* trilogy (2001–2003), the *Spy Kids* franchise (2001–2003), the *Harry Potter* franchise (2001–2007), the *Spiderman* franchise (2002–2007), *Charlie and the Chocolate Factory* (2005) and the *Fantastic Four* movies (2005–2007).

Animation: *The Iron Giant* (1999), *Atlantis: The Lost Empire* (2001) and *Lilo & Stitch* (2002).

Hollywood's Addiction to Computer Generated Images (CGI)

CGI and other special effects have the power of bringing to the big screen a *truth* that does not exist in the real world. This is a significant component to creating science-fiction-fantasy films in the twenty-first century, because suspension of the audience's disbelief is an absolute necessity to achieve success in this film genre. The audience must *forget* that what they're watching will not and cannot happen. They must be able to put themselves in the characters' predicament and feel their emotions.

Indeed, computer-generated effects are a key part of a film's marketing campaign. "Money shots" (creative scenes that are expensive to film) are routinely requested nearly a year prior to a film's release to power a trailer. "You can't underestimate the marketing component of visual effects," says Chris DeFaria, senior vice president of physical production and special effects at Warner. "When you have something key to communicating a movie, like the wave in *The Day After Tomorrow*, you have to get it done in time for the teaser."[8]

It almost goes without saying that if you write an intriguing science-fiction-fantasy screenplay you'll increase the odds of selling it. And the prospect of using special effects—especially those generated by a digital environment—*must* be a huge selling point. This film genre, by default, is a big-budget one. By and large, studios don't want to cut corners and end up with a cheesy-looking film. So it's important for you as the screenwriter to max out your imagination and go beyond what can be done through live action or mechanically created special effects.

Even though the new buzzword in special effects is "blended cinema"—a combination of live action and animation in a single shot[9]—prosthetics and makeup remain important elements in science-fiction-fantasy because every effect simply can't be computer generated; at least, not yet. It's still almost a requirement that you create visuals and sequences in your screenplay that necessitate the use of computer-generated images. Also, note that all of the most popular sci-fi films incorporate the same storytelling components as the action-adventure genre.

Figure 4.3   *2005–2007 Top Box Office Science-Fiction-Fantasy Films*[10]

2007

- *Spiderman 3*
- *Transformers*
- *Pirates of the Caribbean: At World's End*
- *Harry Potter and the Order of the Phoenix*
- *I Am Legend*
- *Alvin and the Chipmunks*
- *Fantastic Four: Rise of the Silver Surfer*

2006

- *Pirates of the Caribbean: Dead Man's Chest*
- *X-Men: The Last Stand*
- *Superman Returns*
- *Click*

2005

- *Star Wars: Episode III—Revenge of the Sith*
- *The Chronicles of Narnia: The Lion, the Witch and the Wardrobe*
- *War of the Worlds*
- *King Kong*
- *Charlie and the Chocolate Factory*
- *Batman Begins*
- *Robots*

Choose What to Write

It's important to note that most science-fiction-fantasy films are adaptations from previously existing material, such as novels, short stories and comics. In the attempt to produce a fresh film in this genre, Stephen Spielberg's DreamWorks Pictures started developing a film in 2007 based on the graphic novel *Cowboys and Aliens* for Paramount Studios.[11] These types of films are *adaptations*. The idea of creating a new mythology in film is akin to salmon swimming upstream to mate. In fact, the industry views "original mythology" as a very risky enterprise, because science-fiction-fantasy films are expensive to produce. Therefore, the marketers—departments at studios that work together to sell films to audiences, and that have a lot of say in what gets developed and produced—are going to look for built-in selling elements or devices before signing off on a film development slate. This is an important reason why sequels and film franchises are an important part of a studio's business model.

About now you're probably asking yourself: "Why do I have to worry about how my screenplay in film form will be marketed?" The answer is that you have to worry about it because the people who buy screenplays worry about it! The easier you make it for them to see the possibilities, the stronger your chances of selling your screenplay. It's important never to lose sight of the fact that you're writing for a *business*.

One approach is to do a *gap analysis*: look at what hasn't been made for a while within popular sub-genres—there are websites containing past years' box office results—and write a screenplay to fill that gap. But at the top of the list is the science-fiction-action-thriller.

Do the "Heavy Lifting"

Because imagination and creativity are so important to science-fiction-fantasy storytelling, it's crucial to do your homework. The time you spend creating the various elements of your science-fiction-fantasy will reward you tremendously during the actual writing of the screenplay. So, roll up your sleeves and let's get started!

Heavy Lifting & the Fairytales

My "spec" science-fiction-fantasy screenplay is a contemporized version of Goldilocks and the Three Bears. The fairytale is about a little girl who finds an empty house that belongs to three bears. She breaks in and makes herself at home. After damaging their property and sampling their cuisine, she climbs into each of their beds and eventually dozes off in one. Then Papa, Mama and Baby Bear return home, find her and eat her.

In this chapter, I will share with you the development process for this idea as I review how to write for the science-fiction-fantasy genre.

Science-Fiction-Fantasy & Casting

In the past, unknown and not-too-talented actors tended to star in science-fiction-fantasy films. However, it's become much more likely today to see A-list actors such as Tom Cruise and Will Smith headlining science-fiction-fantasy casts. That's because many of these films fall under the category of big-budget tentpole movies. (See Chapter 2 for more on this.) Sometimes well-known actors who aren't big box office draws emerge as such after starring in a science-fiction film. *The Matrix's* Keanu Reeves and *The Terminator's* Arnold Schwarzenegger are perfect examples of this phenomenon.

As is true in every popular film genre, it benefits the screenwriter to create an interesting hero and villain in order to attract star-level actors to your project.

Develop Science-Fiction-Fantasy Heroes & Villains

The centerpiece of a science-fiction-fantasy story is a powerful villain who also evokes sympathy and pity from the audience. This is true because the threat to man or society is what brings the fear factor to this genre's storytelling. No matter what, your characters must act rationally. Equally important, the hero must not be passive or "super"—unless, of course, the hero is actually a superhero. One of your goals as a writer is to create three-dimensional characters with whom the audience can identify. This means creating a primary relationship outside the mainplot of fighting the villain, such as a love story. This love story need not be sexual, and can revolve around family relationships or friendships or both.

One key characteristic of the science-fiction-fantasy hero is that he or she is not concerned with self-preservation, and so is *noble*. In *Star Wars*, Luke Skywalker's (Mark Hamill) unselfish goal is to save the universe from the likes of Darth Vader (David Prowse, voice by James Earl Jones), though he began the adventure seeking only to save Princess Leia (Carrie Fisher) from the dark one. In *War of the Worlds* (2005), Ray Ferrier (Tom Cruise) only wants to keep his son and daughter alive in the face of world annihilation—his safety is not an issue as he learns the value of being a good father. Bruce Wayne (Christian Bale) uses the disguise of Batman in *Batman Begins* (2005) to save a decaying Gotham City from the criminals who prey upon the innocent, even though he started out only seeking revenge for his parents' senseless murder. The interesting thing about Batman is that he has no superpowers, which makes him highly identifiable to the audience.

Take the time to sketch out the physical, social and psychological profiles for all your major characters. (Use Appendix A: *Character Development Template* if you need help.)

Choose Your Hero

My Goldilocks is *Mollie Stryker*. She oversteps her authority and just about ruins a suspect's life. I'm using the image of Christina Ricci (*Cursed* [2005] and *Black Snake Moan* [2007]) for the protagonist because she has certain intensity, having successfully emerged from her peculiar image established in the *Addams Family* films. I can also see her playing sexual ambivalence very well, which is an important component of my story. Here's her thumbnail sketch:

> *Mollie Stryker* (thirty) is young for a police officer, but intense. A realist and a cynic, she's tough-minded, no-nonsense, lonely and grappling with her sexual identity. Right now, her social life is her job. She heads up a Special Missing Persons Unit, created under political pressure because of the serial disappearances of children. Before this assignment, she worked on family abuse cases. She has a master's degree in social work and a bachelor's in criminology.

Her co-antagonist, *Victor* (Papa Bear), will, over the course of the story, evolve to a co-protagonist. I'm using the image of Jake Gyllenhaal (*The Day After Tomorrow* [2004] and *Zodiac*[2007]) because he has the right demeanor for this character. Here's his thumbnail sketch:

> *Victor James* (forty) is a forensic attorney who specializes in finding missing children. Mild-mannered and easygoing, he shuns the limelight. He's a workaholic who has little time for relationships. He met Mollie while working on a case. They had a sexual relationship and it ended badly. He believes that aliens exist; in his words, "If we're the superior beings in the universe, man, we are in deep trouble."

Mollie's other co-antagonist is *Liz*, the Mama Bear. It's her personal life that Mollie invades and rips apart. I'm using the image of Carrie-

Anne Moss (*The Matrix* franchise) because Trinity's sensibilities (minus the amazing superpowers) are exactly how I see this character. Here's her thumbnail sketch:

> For *Liz Rhodes* (forty) the unexpected death of her husband shattered her life. As she's on the verge of a nervous breakdown, her teenage daughter begins to act out. When accused of murdering her own child, Liz becomes the latest victim of the media frenzy surrounding the serial disappearances of children. She grows from a victim into strong a mother.

Blair is my Baby Bear. I'm using the image of Dakota Fanning (*Man on Fire* [2004] and *War of the Worlds* [2005]), even though this character is a tad older. It's Fanning's maturity as an actress that I'm drawing upon during the writing process. Here's her thumbnail sketch:

> *Blair Rhodes* (sixteen) is a handful. Though naturally pretty, she's dressing sleazy, abusing drugs and alcohol, and chasing horny boys. She's rebelling against her mother—whose parenting style flip-flops between overbearing and laissez-faire—since her father, who spoiled her rotten, died of prostate cancer. Since her father's death, Blair's been in and out of rehabilitation programs.

Give Your Hero a Strong Goal

Mollie must stop the serial kidnapping of children. This goal gets more and more complicated as the story progresses.

Choose Your Villain

It doesn't take a genius to realize that the villains of popular sci-fi and fantasy films mostly come from other worlds. They're creatures, aliens, viruses, robots. Those who are human are variations on human: Doc Ock (*Spiderman 2*), for example, is part man and part machine.

The aliens are the bad guys in this story.

Make Your Villain Three-Dimensional

More often than not, screenwriters forget to give their villains emotionally identifiable traits. While this character's role is to thwart your hero or heroine, you still want the audience to connect with him or her on some level. And of course, the more interesting the villain, the stronger potential there will be to attract a well-known actor.

Give Your Villain a Strong Goal

In my story, it's a very simple but necessary goal: survival of their species, which is stranded on earth.

Develop Your Sci-Fi Premise

As is true for most Hollywood studio films, creating a high-concept premise is enormously important to attracting interest in your screenplay. To review—high concept means that the premise's *situation* is more important than its *characters*. Specifically, aliens rising from beneath the earth to take over the world in *War of the Worlds*, the world held captive in virtual reality enforced by the megalomaniac Mr. Smith in *The Matrix*, or a magical world that can only be accessed through a wardrobe closet in *The Chronicles of Narnia: The Lion, The Witch and the Wardrobe*. These are all high-concept situations.

The basic premise for Goldilocks and the Three Bears is:

> *When a curious little girl on a walk through the woods comes across a house where no one is at home, she breaks in, eats their food and sleeps in their beds, only to be eaten when the house's owners—the three bears—return.*

My high-concept contemporary sci-fi retelling of this fairytale is:

> *A female Seattle cop—caught in the throes of a sexual identity crisis—teams up with a male forensic attorney to find a mother's missing daughter, discovers the kidnappers are not of this world and finds her life in danger as she works to stop them from abducting troubled teenagers.*

Choose a Fascinating Title

My title for this screenplay is *Snatched!*

Choose Your Sci-Fi Theme

It's universally agreed upon that the central theme for science-fiction storytelling goes to the core fears of the human subconscious. On a realistic level, these fears include massive war, doomsday weapons, disease plagues and, as the twenty-first century proceeds, genetic engineering. On a more overactive-imagination level, the fears include such things as alien and robot invasions, alternative worlds, virtual reality, time travel and paradoxes.

When you really think about it, you can sum up all of these themes under the umbrella of "fear of the unknown." Religion also plays an important thematic role in science-fiction-fantasy storytelling. While it was perhaps done unintentionally (though experts doubt it), C.S. Lewis' *Chronicles of Narnia* is filled with Christian allegories. And don't forget that the *Star Wars* films have at their core a power referred to as "the force" which embraces the concept of the power of faith.

The dramatic leap from Goldilocks and the Three Bears to *Snatched!* is primarily a thematic one, but with a twist. I started out writing a drama about children being kidnapped for the purpose of harvesting their organs. It was a very dark story, and in fact was too dark for my agent and producers. In order to make the story's problem more acceptable to a wider audience, I made the primary villains aliens, and thus my very dark drama became science-fiction-fantasy.

The themes of Goldilocks and the Three Bears are self-preservation and concern for law and order, that is, respect for the property of others.[12] The lesson of the story is to think about how your actions might hurt others. I essentially shifted the lesson of Goldilocks respecting the belongings of others from property to something more emotionally identifiable for an audience—children.

For me, the theme of *Snatched!* works on two levels: personal and cultural, or sexual identity and survival of mankind through its youth. So the concern for the property of others is connected to one's child. And the survival of the alien species is connected to the survival of the human species.

Sci-Fi Storytelling: Structure & Plot

When it comes to writing science-fiction-fantasy, screenwriters need to go beyond the standard screenwriting staples of three-dimensional characters, captivating plotlines and interesting story arcs. You must create an entirely unique world in just over one hundred pages.[13] This is a tall order indeed. However, it's certainly a very necessary ambition if you want your screenplay to have commercial value. This may be an important reason why many sci-fi films are adaptations of short stories and novels, or why so many are remakes and sequels. In fact, all but one of the top box office hits in Figure 4.2—the animated *Robots*—fall into this category. Because originality is so valuable in this genre, re-creating reality is not paramount. In fact, verisimilitude is not an issue in science fiction; suspension of disbelief is supreme.[14]

This means that you must take the audience away from what is real by creating a *new* reality. Often the new reality is an extrapolation of what the audience already knows or believes to be true. Sending a man to the moon begat *Star Trek*. In this case, science fiction merges the science into the story, rather than using it as a prop or putting it on display.[15]

In an interview, George Lucas, the creator of the *Star Wars* franchise, said in essence that visual effects are meant to create a sense of a new reality and should not be held on the screen too long just because they're expensive or wonderful to behold. His point is that the visual effects should serve the storytelling, and not vice versa.

Key Elements of the Sci-Fi Story & Plot

Create clear rules. Make the rules of the world you create clear to the audience. Set up and create the world as you tell a compelling story.

Use current social issues. Make your premise and story parallel to current social and political issues. Your story should reflect the fear of contemporary times in some way.

Create suspense. This involves the audience anticipating what's around every corner by playing on the fears of the human unconscious. Suspense is vicarious, so it's important to involve three-dimensional characters so the audience can identify with them.

Use the three prime ingredients. There are three ingredients in fantasy: (1) a sympathetic and likable person whom the audience cares about, (2) chills before tension and (3) the fantasy itself.[16]

Create a unique world for your setting. Ideally, something that's hasn't been seen before in film.

Select a type of "alien." There are two different kinds of aliens: those from other planets and those from the world we live in.

Use Mythic Structure as a Guide

When writing science-fiction-fantasy screenplays, screenwriters often use Joseph Campbell's Heroes Journey. This was discussed in Chapter 2, but here is a reminder of the twelve stages of the Hero's Journey:[17]

1. Ordinary World

2. Call to Adventure
3. Refusal of the Call
4. Meeting with the Mentor
5. Crossing the First Threshold
6. Test, Allies, Enemies
7. Approach to the Inmost Cave
8. Ordeal
9. Reward (Seizing the Sword)
10. The Road Back
11. Resurrection
12. Return with the Elixir

The Five Essential Elements of Science-Fiction-Fantasy Storytelling

After having viewed many science-fiction-fantasy films, I've found that most, if not all, utilize five essential elements. These are:

Create a threat. What is it that plays on the audience's fears and terror of the unknown? In the film *Alien* (1979), for example, this threat is obviously the indestructible alien monster.

Provide an expert. The audience needs to understand the science of the story, whether it is accurate to the real world or "movie science," so include someone in your script who can explain it to them. In *Alien*, this is the ship's scientist, who turns out to be a highly sophisticated android, Ash (Ian Holm), working in the interest of the corporation.

Create emotional jeopardy. You must bring humanity to the story and, more often than not, involve an emotional relationship between the protagonist and a subplot antagonist. In *Alien*, this is the relationship between Ripley (Sigourney Weaver) and Dallas (Tom Skerritt).

Offer a demonstration. You must clearly express the danger that the unknown poses to human beings in a way the audience can identify with. In *Alien*, when the baby alien bursts out of the first victim's stomach, it's a clear indication that this species intends to use human bodies as incubators. As the story unfolds, other deadly forms of harm demonstrate menace, such as the alien blood that burns through steel.

Offer a lesson. What is the universal theme of the story? More often than not, you should address the foibles of humankind. In *Alien*, the use of Ash as an android offers a clear warning: corporations can and will betray their employees for the almighty dollar. In the end, Ridley triumphs over the alien to establish that humans are ultimately the superior beings in the universe. Since the heroine and the alien are both female, there is an additional, deeper lesson offered: women will do whatever it takes to protect their young.

Figure 4.4   *The Five Essential Elements in* Star Wars

1. *The threat:* The Empire led by Grand Moff Tarkin and Darth Vader
2. *The expert:* Ben Obi-Wan Kenobi
3. *The emotional jeopardy:* Princess Leia Organa
4. *The demonstration:* The Death Star blows up Leia's home planet
5. *The lesson:* Man triumphs over machine because man has religion (believes in something more powerful than himself, i.e., the force)

Combine the five essential elements with your story and its structure and you're on your way to writing a strong, commercial science-fiction-fantasy screenplay. Here are the five essential elements for *Snatched!*:

1. *The threat:* Aliens kidnapping children to use their organs
2. *The expert:* Victor James, forensic attorney specializing in children's abduction and believer in aliens
3. *The emotional jeopardy:* Blair, Liz's daughter who is kidnapped by aliens
4. *The demonstration:* Kidnapping children through a network of youth camps
5. *The lesson:* Children are our future, and we must love and protect them

Snatched!: *Story & Plot*

Because I've already written this screenplay, I'm demonstrating an expanded story and mainplot with the central love story, all structured into a three-act treatment.

Act One

The "Hook" (Opening Sequence)

A spaceship wings itself to earth and crash-lands in a Canadian forest. The year is 1944. *Mollie Stryker*, a handsome woman with the demeanor of a pit bull, crashes into a sleazy motel looking for a suspect. The time is present day. It looks like the perp is long gone until he opens fire from a closet, shooting Molly several times. All the cops open fire and turn the shooter into a mess of bloody flesh. A bullet-proof vest saves Mollie.

The Story's Problem

Liz and her teenage daughter, *Blair*, fight over boys and Blair's sleazy dressing habits while shopping in the mall. Blair mysteriously disappears after we see a *Tall Stranger* lurking around the mall's parking lot. Mollie, head of Seattle's Special Missing Persons Unit, questions Liz as part of her investigation of an epidemic of missing teens. Mollie and Liz instantly clash when Mollie informs Liz that she's a suspect in her own daughter's disappearance.

The Problem Gets Worse for the Protagonist

As the media criticizes Liz, we learn that her husband recently died, and this has added to her estrangement from Blair. Mollie is convinced that Liz killed Blair in a burst of anger and hid her body. But as Mollie investigates, she gets to know Liz better and, in an ironic twist, finds herself attracted to her. This stirs Mollie's ongoing sexual identity crisis. After trying to help Liz find her daughter—to no avail—Mollie becomes convinced Liz is telling the truth.

The Protagonist's Moral Dilemma

Mollie needs help. She brings in her ex-boyfriend, *Victor*—a handsome forensic attorney whose specialty is finding missing children—for help. Mollie figures if he can solve his five missing-children cases, which would now include Blair, it will help Mollie solve the dozens of cases on her plate.

Act Two

Protagonist Gains Ground

In another emotional twist, Victor *also* finds himself falling for Liz, and he begins competing with his ex-girlfriend for the distraught mother's affections. He's a sucker for fallen angels.

But Victor and Mollie clash when he tells her he thinks that aliens are kidnapping the missing Seattle teenagers. Mollie plays along, helping Victor on a lead, but the only "alien" she finds is a Canadian doctor who makes his living finding organs for transplants. Another promising lead takes Victor, Mollie and Liz to Vancouver where they find a lukewarm trail to a Youth Club camp in a remote Canadian forest. When they arrive, things look suspicious, but still there is no sign of Blair or any wrongdoing. Mollie decides the camp looks too perfect and plans a break-in. They find children's clothes . . . and among them is Blair's purse. Liz goes into panic mode. They search and find an operating room with instruments that are clearly not manmade. They also find Blair locked in a dark room all alone. Mother and daughter are reunited.

Protagonist Loses Ground

Now convinced there's foul play, Mollie and Victor decide they must rescue the kids at the camp. They successfully snatch the kids from the camp, but in a wild chase by a helicopter that contains two *Tall Alien Humanoids*, they are run off the road. Mollie, Liz, Victor, Blair and the liberated kids hike their way through the Canadian forest, determined to get to the U.S. border. Along the way, a kid nearly drowns in the river and Mollie and Victor have to come to terms with their affections for Liz. In a tender moment, Mollie accepts that she's not bisexual but a lesbian and she gives Victor her blessing to pursue Liz, who is heterosexual.

All Is Lost

As the group hikes for the border, they come across the alien spaceship that crash-landed in 1944. Inside is the same operating room and instruments they found at the camp. The missing children have died . . .

Everyone is distraught and no one knows what to do, but the humanoid aliens' helicopter swooping down on them again makes the decision for them. A group of stone-throwing Canadian Aboriginals chases off the helicopter. The Aboriginals escort the group to the U.S. border.

Act Three

Protagonist Recommits to the Original Goal

On the short flight back to Seattle, Liz demands that Mollie and Victor do something more, because she doesn't want to see any more children hurt. But Victor and Mollie are convinced that no one will believe their story.

Climax

Back in Seattle, the two Tall Alien Humanoids attack Blair in her bedroom but—surprise!—it's not Blair in the bed, it's Mollie. She shoots one alien humanoid while Victor fights the other when he tries to attack Liz in her bed. But Liz isn't there either! A late-night visit from the FBI takes away the remaining alien humanoid. The agents warn Victor and Mollie not to reveal the existence of the aliens. The grim truth is that the organs of missing teens have kept the Little Grays alive all these years. We learn that these humanoids are the protectors of a species of Gray Aliens that the government has been trying to find for nearly fifty years. Mollie and Victor lie about seeing the spaceship. Mollie organizes a surprise bust of a cargo freighter that has been transporting the missing teenagers to Canada and finds some of them still alive. Mollie returns the missing children with a cover story. Victor and Liz are in love and she joins his practice to help find missing children. Blair begins to reconcile with her mother. Mollie finds the local TV news reporter is attracted to her.

Denouement

The story ends with Mollie, Victor and Liz secretly returning to the hidden spaceship and blowing it to smithereens. But we see the Little Gray aliens had already left the ship as they hike through the forest . . .

The Sci-Fi Writing Style

Many of the same devices used in suspense are used in writing science-fiction-fantasy. The use of shadows, sound effects and creating an eerie subtext are vital to effective sci-fi writing. The screenwriter should provide the tone and atmosphere—a blueprint from which the director, cinematographer and composer can begin to do their jobs. Use language that creates rich visual and auditory imagery. Here are some examples.

James Cameron sets the tone early in *Aliens* screenplay (1986):

```
SOMETIME IN THE FUTURE - SPACE
Silent and endless. The stars shine like the love
of God . . . cold and remote. Against them drifts a
tiny chip of technology.
```

Larry and Andy Wachowski quickly take the reader into the world of *The Matrix* in their 1997 screenplay:

```
ON COMPUTER SCREEN
So close it has no boundaries.
A blinking cursor pulses in the electronic darkness
like a heart coursing with phosphorous light, burn-
ing beneath the derma of black-neon glass.
```

Who could stop reading after those opening lines?

Fran Walsh, Philippa Boyens and Peter Jackson ominously set up the world the characters are entering in their *King Kong* screenplay (2005):

```
Beyond the great wall, SKULL ISLAND is like no
place you've ever seen before . . .

The VOLCANIC ROCKS form a JAGGED, TORTURED LAND-
SCAPE of DEEP CREVASSES and TOWERING CLIFFS. The
vegetation is THICK, the JUNGLE DARK. ANCIENT
GNARLED TREES twist out of the ground, thick LICHEN
and long MOSSES hang from branches and TANGLED
VINES. STEAM RISES from festering SWAMPS.
```

Dean Devlin and Roland Emmerich describe the destructive force of the alien ship in their screenplay for *Independence Day* (1996) like this:

```
As the light amplifies, the believers chant, louder
and louder. Suddenly the white light DISAPPEARS.
The believers are stunned. In a brief moment it is
replaced with a BLAST.

A DESTRUCTION BEAM BLASTS down onto the rooftop,
splintering everything there, police helicopter
included, into a billion tiny particles.
```

Finally, here's a longer writing style sample from my "spec" sci-fi screenplay *Snatched!* that takes the story back to what was revealed in the opening sequence:

EXT. CANADIAN FOREST - DAY

The expedition hikes through the thick woods.

Victor leads the way, Liz by his side, tiring.

Mollie's still going strong, her eyes searching the surrounding trees for any sign of danger.

Blair's with the other children—they're exhausted too.

Then Victor's eyes lock on something up ahead. He stares in awe at—

The huge crashed spaceship, now overgrown with foliage, has nearly become a part of the forest.

The expedition stands behind Victor, in awe, dwarfed by the big vessel.

> MOLLIE
>
> My God.

> LIZ
>
> This has been here a long time.

> VICTOR
>
> That's at least thirty or forty years
> of growth.

They approach the spaceship. It looms over them.

Mollie searches and finds a crack in the hull, draws her Lady Smith .38 like the cop she is.

> VICTOR
>
> What are you doing?

> MOLLIE
>
> You stay here with the kids.

Before Victor can object, Mollie slips through the crack.

INT. SPACESHIP - DAY

Mollie's flashlight beam cuts through the darkness— on the bulkheads are the same peculiar symbols found at the day camp.

She raises her gun as she skulks through a—

Maze of badly damaged corridors.

She finally comes upon—

A menacing light straight ahead: it warns of peril but she does not stop.

INT. OPERATING ROOM - SPACESHIP - DAY

Mollie moves in, shines the light: it's the same as the one from the day camp:

White.

Stainless steel.

Bright work lights.

On the operating table—

A GRAY ALIEN:

Small.

The size of a 10-year-old.

And dead.

It looks like an operation was interrupted: there's a gaping incision.

Mollie is stupefied. Then she sees—

Something move in the shadows. She grits her teeth, points the light and the gun at:

Several GRAY ALIENS huddled together. They squint when light hits them.

                    MOLLIE
          Freeze!

Keeping her Lady Smith steady, Mollie moves closer. The increasing strength of the beam causes the Gray Aliens to block their eyes. They shiver, cower, then—

Mollie drops her gun—grabs her head in excruciating pain!

                    MOLLIE
          Stop it! Stop it!

Mollie can't stand it another second, runs out, leaving her weapon behind.

EXT. PARTIAL CLEARING - CANADIAN FOREST - DAY

Mollie bursts out of the crack in the spaceship, her eyes bulging to the size of quarters.

Victor runs to her:

                    VICTOR
          What happened?

Mollie settles down as the pain subsides.

> MOLLIE
> Aliens. Little gray guys.

> VICTOR
> What?

> MOLLIE
> Like on THE X-FILES.

The distant whooping of helicopter blades stops the next question.

Abject fear sweeps the children as they search the pale blue sky.

> VICTOR
> Everybody follow me. Stay close and try
> to keep up.

Victor heads around the spaceship. Liz, Mollie and the children in his wake.

And they are quickly swallowed up by the surrounding woods...

EXT. WOODS - CANADA - DAY

The expedition snakes through the vegetation. The children, propelled by their fear, have no problem keeping up.

Overhead—the whoop of the helicopter grows near.

The expedition stays on course as the helicopter screams past above them.

Victor and the group hit the edge of the tree line and move into a—

EXT. CLEARING - CANADIAN FOREST - DAY

The helicopter gently sets down. The Twin Tall Strangers slip out—still armed with the technologically advanced weapons.

The expedition stops cold—the prop wash from the helicopter nearly blowing them off their feet.

Out of nowhere—

Rocks the size of golf balls rain down on the Twin Tall Strangers—they are hit and hurt.

The stones hammer the helicopter's fragile hull as the Twin Tall Strangers scramble back inside.

The helicopter promptly lifts off—streaks away into the sky.

More than fifty Canadian Aboriginals emerge from the woods and surround the expedition—the Indian Fisherboy among them.

> ABORIGINAL LEADER
> Allez! Tu es perdu?

> BLAIR
> Oui.

> MOLLIE
> Tell him we have to get to the United States border.

> BLAIR
> Uh . . . Nous voudrons aller à les États-Unis.

> ABORIGINAL LEADER
> Suivez. Vite!

The Aboriginals head toward the tree line, the expedition follows.

> VICTOR
> What happened inside that ship?

> MOLLIE
> Let's just say you were right.

> VICTOR
> About what?

> MOLLIE
> Everything.

Off Victor's curious stare...

Figure 4.5 *Writers Guild of America's Greatest Sci-Fi Screenplays*[18]

- *Back to the Future* (written by Robert Zemeckis and Bob Gale)
- *E.T.: The Extra-terrestrial* (written by Melissa Mathison)
- *Star Wars* (written by George Lucas)

Science-Fiction-Fantasy & Television Series

Many of the movie serials of the 1940s and 1950s were science-fiction-fantasy, and led in to early science-fiction television, which produced such programs as *Tom Corbett: Space Cadet* and *Captain Video*. The *Twilight Zone* was the first successful TV series that included sci-fi for adults, but it often blurred the distinction between science fiction and fantasy. *Star Trek* was groundbreaking in that it introduced a wider audience to the tropes of real science fiction. Since the revival of *Star Trek: The Next Generation* in 1988, there has always been at least one major science-fiction series on television.[19]

Science-Fiction-Fantasy on TV

Here's a recap of some of the most popular science fiction television series, decade-by-decade.[20]

In the 1950s, there was *Captain Video & His Video Rangers* (1949–1955), *Adventures of Superman* (1952–1958), *Flash Gordon* (1954–1955), *Captain Midnight* (1954–1958), *One Step Beyond* (1959–1961) and *The Twilight Zone* (1959–1964, remade in 1985–1989 and 2002–2003).

The 1960s saw such favorites as *The Outer Limits* (1963–1965), *My Favorite Martian* (1963–1966), *Lost in Space* (1965–1968), *I Dream of Jeannie* (1965–1970) and the original *Star Trek* series (1966–1969).

In the 1970s, these sci-fi series hit the small screen: *Land of the Lost* (1974–1977), *The Bionic Woman* (1976–1978), *The Incredible Hulk* (1978–1982) and *Fantasy Island* (1978–1984).

The 1980s aired *Knight Rider* (1982–1986), *Star Trek: The Next Generation* (1987–1994), *Alien Nation* (1989–1990) and *Quantum Leap* (1989–1993).

Sci-fi maintained a steady popularity on television in the 1990s with *Highlander* (1992–1998), *Lois & Clark: The New Adventures of Superman* (1993–1997), *Star Trek: Deep Space Nine* (1993–1999), *The X-Files* (1993–2002), *Babylon 5* (1994–1998), *Star Trek: Voyager* (1995–2001), *Earth: Final Conflict* (1997–2002), *Stargate SG-1* (1997–present) and *Charmed* (1998–2006).

As the twenty-first century unfolds, the Sci-Fi Channel has emerged as a primary destination for television viewers looking for their fix of science-fiction-fantasy. Much of the programming is syndicated series, but there's an ongoing substantial investment in original programming. Here are the top science-fiction-fantasy television series for the first decade of this century: *Farscape* (1999–2003), *Adromeda* (2000–2005), *Smallville* (2001–present), *The 4400* (2004–present), *Battlestar Gallatica* (2004–2008 [remake of the 1978–1979 series]), Lost (2004–present), *Supernatural* (2005–present), *Kyle XY* (2006–present), *Eureka* (2006–present) and *Heroes* (2006–present).

Your Assignment

"There is a fifth dimension beyond that which is known to man. It is a dimension as vast as space and as timeless as infinity. It is the middle ground between light and shadow, between science and superstition, and it lies between the pit of man's fears and the summit of his knowledge. This is the dimension of imagination. It is an area which we call the *Twilight Zone.*"[21]

It's your turn to travel in your own imagination and develop a science-fiction-fantasy screenplay. Use Appendix D: *Science-Fiction-Fantasy Worksheet* as a guide.

May the force be with you.

Notes

1. James Gunn, *The Science of Science-Fiction Writing* (Lanham, MD: The Scarecrow Press, Inc., 2000), 72–73.

2. Ibid, 91.

3. Wikipedia, "Science Fiction," *http://en.wikipedia.org/wiki/Science_fiction* (accessed February 14, 2006).

4. Ibid.

5. Tim Dirks, "Science Fiction Films," *www.filmsite.org/sci-fifilms2.html* (accessed February 15, 2006).

6. *Planet Stories* was a pulp science-fiction magazine published by Fiction House; seventy-one monthly issues appeared between 1939 and 1955. It featured a particular kind of romantic, swashbuckling adventure in a science-

fiction context, and was renowned for its colorful covers, typically featuring a young woman in (for the time) rather scanty apparel. Source: http://en.wikipedia.org/wiki/Planet_Stories (accessed March 31, 2007).

7. Wikipedia, "Science Fiction," *http://en.wikipedia.org/wiki/Science_fiction* (accessed February 14, 2006).

8. David S. Cohen and Ben Fritz, "More Bucks for F/X Bangs: Studio's Continuing Appetite for CGI Shots Leads to Bigger-budgeted Pix," *www.variety.com*, Sep. 4, 2005.

9. David S. Cohen, "Harmonic Convergence: Blended Cinema Pics Engage Filmmakers from Both Live Action and Animation," *Daily Variety*, February 15, 2006, A1.

10. 2005–2007 Domestic Grosses from *www.boxofficemojo.com* (accessed June 19, 2007).

11. Michael Flemming, "D'Works, U Saddle Up 'Cowboys'," Daily Variety, June 21, 2007. The creators of *Cowboys and Aliens* were also involved in developing *Men in Black* (1997) and *Transformers* (2007) for the big screen.

12. Jan Brett, "Goldilocks and the Three Bears." Good Media, Good Kids, University of Notre Dame, *http://goodmedia.nd.edu/reviews/review.cfm?id=1539* (accessed June 19, 2007).

13. Josh Spector, "Hollywood Roundtable: Science Fiction & Fantasy Films," *Creative Screenwriting* magazine, July/August 2005, 61.

14. James Gunn, *The Science of Science-Fiction Writing* (Latham, MD: The Scarecrow Press, Inc., 2000), 103.

15. J.N. Williamson (ed.), *How to Write Tales of Horror, Fantasy & Science Fiction* (Cincinnati, OH: Writer's Digest Books, 1987), 87.

16. Ibid, 65.

17. Christopher Vogler, *The Writer's Journey: Mythic Structure for Writers* (Studio City, CA: Michael Weise Productions, 1998), 14.

18. Source: The Writers Guild of America, West, "The 101 Greatest Screenplays." The list can be found at *www.wga.org*.

19. Wikipedia, "Science Fiction," *http://en.wikipedia.org/wiki/Science_fiction* (accessed February 14, 2006).

20. Source: *www.tv.com*.

21. "The Twilight Zone," opening narration for 1959 Season 1 by Rod Serling from *www.imdb.com/title/tt0052520/quotes* (accessed June 25, 2007).

5

The Horror-Fantasy Genre

The Fear Factor

```
FADE IN:

INT. CHAMBER #1 - NIGHT

The handsome face of a teen boy, 18, sleeping. A
sweet smile plays over DAVID'S lips, then—

He sits up and SCREAMS at the top of his lungs!

He's on a cot, the walls unpainted cement brick.
The only other piece of furniture is a hefty:

Execution-style oak chair; gruesome-looking with
arm and leg straps.

David settles, his breathing slows down, he seems
to remember where he is, looks at the:

Small six-inch porthole in the steel door. It's
closed. He waits as if expecting someone to open
it. Nothing. He lays back onto the cot. Closes his
eyes. But sleep doesn't come.

INT. HALLWAY - NIGHT

Dark. Silent. The bare light bulbs cast eerie shadows
of—

Someone walking. POV: the unpainted cement brick
walls interrupted by a—

Series of gray steel doors: each small porthole
covered with a door with handles. The Someone stops
at one of the steel doors.
```

David on the cot—his eyes wide, expectant, as the small window opens and closes quickly.

INT. CHAMBER #1 - NIGHT

David listens: keys rattle in the door's lock. He sits up as it creaks open, stares at:

ELIZABETH BABCOCK (40ish), strikingly beautiful but sinister at the same time. She's dressed in all black, goth-style, with dark eye makeup.

> ELIZABETH
> Another nightmare, sweetie?

David's ears perk at—

INT. HALLWAY - NIGHT

The distinctive wobble of warped wheels on a cart moving down the hallway and carrying a hemodialysis machine.

INT. CHAMBER #1 - NIGHT

David's fear is palpable. Just then, the cart with the high-tech gadget rolls inside and—

INT. CHAMBER #2 - NIGHT

David's SCREAM causes ERIN, a cute 18-year-old girl, to cover her ears in abject fear. Bandages cover the veins inside both her forearms.

INT. CHAMBER #3 - NIGHT

SCARLETT, 18, a plain Jane, covers her eyes, the same bandages on her arms.

INT. CHAMBER #4 - NIGHT

JACKSON, 18, African American, a baby face, stares with determination as David's scream echoes. He rips off his bandages in defiance, "bring it on," revealing a track of needle marks.

INT. CHAMBER #1 - NIGHT

Elizabeth smiles at David, snaps in her porcelain vampire fangs.

> ELIZABETH
> (matter-of-fact)
> Feeding time.

```
EXT. SALT LAKE CITY, UTAH - SUNRISE
The golden sun peeks over the distant mountains and
the city sprawls majestically in the valley below . . .
```

In the next sequence, the audience meets the co-protagonists and other key characters in the story. This opening sequence is my promise to the audience that they're going to see a horror movie.

From the writing perspective, horror, science fiction and fantasy pretty much share the same dramatic elements. However, I've written a separate chapter on the horror genre because Hollywood *markets* this genre as separate from science-fiction-fantasy.

Origins of the Horror-Fantasy Genre

In fact, literature puts the three genres (horror, science fiction and fantasy) together. In terms of film, evidence suggests that the term "horror film" did not become widespread until the late 1930s.[1]

Stuart Kaminsky[2] distinguishes horror from science fiction by arguing that "horror films are overwhelmingly concerned with the fear of death and loss of identity in modern society," while, by contrast, "science-fiction films deal with life and the future, not fear of death." He then discusses as horror films a number of titles thought of by many critics as science fiction—notably *It Came from Outer Space* (1953), *The Creature from the Black Lagoon* (1954) and *Invasion of the Body Snatchers* (1956)—demonstrating how tricky it is to identity the genre of certain films.[3]

Regardless, I'll endeavor to address the horror genre as it applies to understanding the key elements you need to master in order to write a commercially viable screenplay.

But first, it's valuable to understand how the horror film genre has evolved over the years. Film historians agree that horror films developed out of a number of sources, including folktales with devil characters, witchcraft, fables, myths, ghost stories, Grand Guignol melodramas, and Gothic or Victorian novels from Europe by way of Mary Shelley or Bram Stoker. In many ways, the expressionistic German silent cinema led the world in films of horror and the supernatural, and established its cinematic vocabulary and style.[4] But the horror film genre has a colorful history that goes back to 1896, with the first film made by French filmmaker

Georges Méliès, titled *Le Manoir du Diable* (*The Devil's Castle*), which contains some elements of later vampire films.

Then came the great horror films of the 1950s: *The Thing from Another World* (1951), *House of Wax* (1953), *Godzilla* (1954), *The Creature from the Black Lagoon* (1954), *Them!* (1954), *Invasion of the Body Snatchers* (1956), *I Was a Teenage Werewolf* (1957), *The Incredible Shrinking Man* (1957), *The Blob* (1958) and *The Fly* (1958). Most of these films, considered B movies, had low budgets. It's important to point out that all of these films dealt with society's fear of the atomic age, making the element of social relevance very important when developing your idea for a horror story. Also note that drive-in theaters—a teenager destination—were key to the distribution of horror films in the 1950s.

In any discussion of horror films, one must highlight Alfred Hitchcock's *Pyscho* (1960), Brian De Palma's *Carrie* (1976)—an adaptation of Stephen King's novel of the same name—and De Palma's *Dressed to Kill* (1980). In the 1970s and 1980s, movies featuring devil-possession emerged as top horror fare, with such films as *The Exorcist* (1973), *The Omen* (1976), *The Amityville Horror* (1979) and *Poltergeist* (1982).

In the 1990s, films such as *The Devil's Advocate* (1997), *End of Days* (1999) and horror fare featuring African Americans, such as *Def by Temptation* (1990), *Candyman* (1992), *Tales from the Hood* (1995), *Vampire in Brooklyn* (1995) and *The Queen of the Damned* (2002), continued the tradition of devil-possession as a worthy subject aimed at a niche-within-a-niche market.

Critics and film historians agree that in contemporary horror, sequels have become a major convention, with film franchises such as *Friday the 13th*, *Nightmare on Elm Street* and *Halloween*. Comedy has also become a significant storytelling element in such films as *Evil Dead*, the *Scream* movies, *I Know What You Did Last Summer* and the *Scary Movie* and *Army of Darkness* franchises.[5]

The celebrated horror characters like Dracula, Frankenstein, the Mummy, the Werewolf and those relentless zombies will no doubt continue to be either the source of or inspiration for new horror film characters. Of special note is the emergence of writer-director-producer M. Night Shyamalan as a prominent figure whose work is influenced by the horror genre.[6] He just about reinvented the genre by adding horror elements to his family drama-thriller *The Sixth Sense* (1999).

As the film industry progresses through the first decade of the twenty-first century, it is evident that the horror genre is alive and well. In 2007, the genre showed some audience fatigue. However, new distribution means, such as the World Wide Web and direct-to-DVD, are picking up the slack from the drop-off on the big screen. Without a doubt, the new Blu-ray format will fuel the sales of the genre in the home video-market.

These new film-delivery opportunities and the fact that horror attracts youthful audiences make this an excellent genre for neophyte screenwriters to begin their professional careers. For example, *Project Greenlight*[7] launched the careers of new screenwriters Patrick Melton and Marcus Dunstan—both only a few years out of film school—with their comedy-horror-thriller *Feast* (2005). A key element to the film's success, though minor in terms of box office receipts, was the short theatrical release and immediate availability of the film on DVD in video stores for both rental and retail sale. Melton and Dunstan have been hired to write the next series of screenplays in the *Saw* franchise and have signed television development deals.

Popular Horror Sub-Genres

While some critics and film historians may find it difficult to define the horror genre succinctly, for the screenwriter, it comes down to four primary sub-genres:

Supernatural (ghost) fantasy: *The Hills Have Eyes* franchise (1977–2007), the *Blade* franchise (1998–2004), *The Sixth Sense* (1999), *Shadow of the Vampire* (2000), the *Final Destination* franchise (2000–2006), *The Ring* franchise (2002–2005), the *Resident Evil* franchise (2002–2007), the *Underworld* franchise (2003,–2006), *Shaun of the Dead* (2004), *Van Helsing* (2004), *Dawn of the Dead* (2004 remake), *The Grudge* franchise (2004–2006), *Corpse Bride* (2005), *Dark Water* (2005), *Silent Hill* (2006) and *Ghost Rider* (2007).

Sci-fi horror-fantasy: *28 Days Later . . .* (2002), *King Kong* (2005) and *28 Weeks Later* (2007).

Neo-horror (slasher) fantasy: *The Texas Chainsaw Massacre* franchise (1974–2006), *The Hill Have Eyes* franchise (1977–2007), the *Saw* franchise (2004–2007) and the *Hostel* franchise (2005–2007).

Neo-horror comedy fantasy: the *Scream* franchise (1996–2000), *I Know What You Did Last Summer* franchise (1997–1998) and the *Scary Movie* franchise (2000–2006).

Figure 5.1   *Top Grossing Horror Films*[8]

- *King Kong* ($217 million)
- *Ghost Rider* ($115 million)
- *Scary Movie 4* ($88 million)
- *Saw II* ($87 million)
- *The Ring Two* ($76 million)
- *The Exorcism of Emily Rose* ($75 million)
- *The Amityville Horror* (2005) ($65 million)
- *Underworld: Evolution* ($62 million)
- *Corpse Bride* ($53 million)
- *Final Destination 3* ($54 million)
- *The Skeleton Key* ($47 million)
- *Hostel* ($47 million)
- *When a Stranger Calls* (2006) ($47 million)
- *Boogeyman* ($46 million)
- *Silent Hill* ($46 million)
- *The Hills Have Eyes* ($41 million)
- *The Fog* ($29 million)
- *House of Wax* ($32 million)

Hollywood's Fascination with Scaring Audiences

Attracting young audiences is an important goal for studios when deciding on the kinds of films that should be on their production slates. Ancillary to this fact is the growing trend of a nexus between video games and the horror genre.

John Carpenter, the revered director of such horror film classics as *Halloween* (1978), *The Fog* (1980) and *The Thing* (1982), says that horror has "always been a staple of movies. It waxes and wanes depending on culture, but right now, it is one of the few [genres] that some call a sure thing. You make them for a budget, you make them frightening enough, and people show up."[9]

More and more, horror films blend computer generated images (CGI) into the horror genre in order to ramp up the scare factor.

Choose What to Write

Conduct what is called a *gap analysis*: look at what hasn't been made for a while within popular sub-genres—there are websites containing past years' box office results—and write a screenplay to fill that gap. But the bottom line with horror-fantasy is to write something that's *scary*. As you survey produced horror films, you'll quickly realize they all have pretty much the same plot. What separates them is the high-concept premise and how well the characters and dialogue are updated.

The growing trend in horror is to add thriller elements to the mix of story and plot. Even the slasher film (neo-horror) has become more sophisticated in its execution.

Heavy Lifting & the Fairytales

For my horror fairytale example, I'm using Hansel and Gretel because the story is inherently horrifying. Here's a synopsis:[10]

> Hansel and Gretel are the children of a poor woodcutter. Fearing starvation, the woodcutter's wife (variously called the children's mother or stepmother), convinces him to lead the children into the forest and abandon them there. Hansel and Gretel hear her plan and gather white pebbles so that they will be able to leave themselves a trail home. After they return, their mother again convinces the woodcutter to abandon them; this time, however, they can only leave a trail of breadcrumbs. This time, the various animals of the woods eat their trail, and Hansel and Gretel become lost.
>
> Lost in the forest, they find a house made of bread (later versions call it gingerbread), with sugar windows, which they begin to eat. The inhabitant of the house, an old woman, invites them in and prepares a feast for them. The woman, however, is a witch who has built the house to entice children to her, so that she may fatten and eat them. She cages Hansel and makes Gretel her servant. While she prepares to cook Hansel,

she tells Gretel to climb into the oven to be sure it is hot enough, but Gretel guesses that the witch intends to bake her, and tricks the witch into climbing into the oven herself, whereupon Gretel closes her in.

Taking jewels from the witch's house, the children set off for home to reunite with their father, whose wife has since died of evilness. "Then all anxiety was at an end, and they lived together in perfect happiness."

As in the previous chapters, I will develop the horror elements using Hansel and Gretel as a template. Let's start with casting.

Horror-Fantasy Casting

One actor who helped pave the way for the acceptance of the horror genre was Lon (Alonso) Chaney, Sr., known as "the man of a thousand faces" because of his transformative, grotesque makeup and acting genius. He was the first American horror-film star. His most famous role is the lead in *The Phantom of the Opera* (1925).

However, studios today are more inclined to cast unknown talent in horror-fantasy films. Note that the biggest box office winner, *King Kong*, has an array of known actors—even Oscar winner Adrien Brody (*The Pianist*, 2002)—but no big box office stars; at the time the movie was made, Naomi Watts and Jack Black were considered up-and-coming actors. *Saw II* has a few familiar faces, but most of the cast are virtual unknowns.

Studios use this approach because in the horror genre the less baggage an actor brings to a role—all the tabloid gossip and on-again, off-again romances, not to mention political and religious proclivities—the more believable the experience will be for the audience. On the other hand, the producers and directors might use an actor whose career is on the wane as "stunt" casting (which means casting an unexpected choice of actor). So, as a screenwriter developing a horror script, it's freeing to understand this thinking, because the real star of a horror film is the combination of fear and special effects.

Horror-Fantasy Heroes & Villains

Choose Your Hero

The hero (or heroine) of a horror film, naturally, is the one the character whom the audience feels closest to. We need that to comfort us while we are being scared out of our wits. It's often a woman who saves the day or survives the horror of the story, because she represents the continuation of the human species. Sometimes it's the tall, dark, rough-around-the-edges handsome male because he represents the ideal of men protecting women and children. The bottom line on horror heroes is to create a character whom the audience can identify with, believe in and look up to. Therefore it's essential for the hero to have the same basic moral values as the audience, or, at the very least, for the audience to learn to respect him or her.

My heroes (co-protagonists) will be the same two from the fairytale. But I've tweaked Hansel's name to *Hanley* to make it more contemporary, and I've updated Gretel to *Gretchen*. I'm not going to use images of established actors for these two lead characters, because most horror films use new or up-and-coming talent and these characters are in their teens. Here are my thumbnail sketches:

> *Hanley Huntington* (seventeen) is a fraternal twin. He's one of the most popular dudes at the private prep school he and his sister attend. He performs well academically and serves as the senior class president. That's his public persona. Those who know him best also know he has a dark side. He has a bad temper and struggles to control it. He deeply resents his father expecting him to be successful in everything he does. And he also resents that more is expected of him than of his sister.
>
> *Gretchen Huntington* (seventeen) is the other twin. She's nearly the complete opposite of Hanley: unpopular, with poor academic discipline and no interest in joining clubs or participating in group activities. She's a loner. Those who know her better—and they are few and far between—know that she has a great sense of humor, though it's dark and crude. Her father spoils her rotten, protects her fiercely and has no expectations for her future. As far as she's concerned, her trust fund will take care of her for the rest of her life.

Give Your Hero a Strong Goal

Hanley and Gretchen must escape captivity or they will surely die.

A Key Pivotal Character

A key pivotal character is the teens' father, *Bradford "Biff" Huntington*. I'm going to imagine Bill Pullman (*Independence Day* [1996] and *The Grudge*

[2004]) since he's recognizable, yet still not considered a big star. Here's his thumbnail sketch:

> *Bradford "Biff" Huntington* (fifty-ish) is a workaholic. As an investment banker, he has his hands in a lot of other people's money. He inherited plenty of money and has made more on his own. He tries hard to create his son, Hanley, in his own image, but the truth is he was a quiet nerd as a teenager, sat on the bench on all the sports teams he joined and never got along well with the ladies. Though he tries to be a good father, he simply works too much. He's on his second marriage; Hanley and Gretchen are products of his first.

Choose Your Villain

When it comes to villains, simply stated, at the core of the horror genre is the "monster." There are three types:

- Human, e.g., the vampire
- Unhuman, e.g., the creature
- Human/Unhuman, e.g., the werewolf

Transformative monsters, such as the werewolf, have high fear appeal because they possess the ability to go from man (or woman) to beast and back. The bottom line for horror villains is to create someone or something that scares the bejesus out of the audience.

In this way, you have a classic duel between good and evil, creating sides for which the audience can cheer and jeer. It should go without saying that the audience should be sympathetic to both character roles. A key to achieving this is to give both the hero and villain likable traits and at least one fatal flaw. The villain generally has some flaw that will ultimately be his or her demise; for example, the werewolf dies by a silver bullet and the vampire turns to dust in sunlight.

The challenge as a writer is how you adapt this concept to your characters in a contemporary issue. In the film *28 Days Later . . .* (2002), the obvious issue is the government's failure to treat and control the AIDS virus. In *Cabin Fever* (also 2002), it's a flesh-eating virus. So, what's the new virus? What's the new vampire? What's the new werewolf? Or what's the new Frankenstein?

My stepmother character from the fairytale is *Isabella Huntington*. She starts out in the story as an antagonist to Hanley and Gretchen and, as the story unfolds, she emerges as a co-villain. The image I'm using for her is of Toni Collette, because she was excellent in *The Sixth Sense* (1999) and is sexy, glamorous and funny. Here's her thumbnail sketch:

> *Isabella Huntington* (late thirties) has been married to Brad for three years. The first year was smooth, but their relationship started going downhill when Gretchen began complaining about Isabella treating her badly. Though it appears that she and Brad are very much in love, they argue a lot. In the last year, the fights have gotten worse. Brad is ready to bury the hatchet and try to renew their marriage. Isabella agrees, and promises to try to be more attentive to Hanley and Gretchen. But there's a dark secret lurking in this family.

In my fairytale conversion, the witch is *Elizabeth Babcock*. I chose to use what appears to be a human villain and then reveal that she's an unhuman villain. I'm imagining Elizabeth Perkins (*The Ring Two* [2005]) for this role, because I feel she can pull off creepy and sexy at the same time. Here's her thumbnail sketch:

> *Elizabeth Babcock* (forty-ish) worships vampires. She heads a cult group that kidnaps teenagers to drink their blood. What nobody involved knows is that Elizabeth is more than a cult worshipper; she's nearly five hundred years old and a real vampire. The day she can become fully human again is approaching; it's a day that only occurs once every five hundred years. She plans to take full advantage of it.

Give Your Villain a Strong Goal

Her ultimate goal is to become fully human again. In the meantime, her goal is to keep a steady supply of human blood at hand and not reveal her true self to anyone. Keeping her secret is what has allowed her to survive for so long.

Develop Your Horror Premise

At the heart of the horror premise is the nightmare or inner fears of mortal human beings. It's that simple. The challenge for you is to come up with a fresh, unique way of spinning this theme.

Legendary horror film writer-director-producer George Romero took his classic premise for *Night of the Living Dead* (1968) and flipped it to create *Land of the Dead* (2005). In that film, the living dead have taken over the world, and the last humans live in a walled city to protect themselves as they come to grips with the situation.[11]

Writer-director-producer Kevin Williamson took the basic elements of a horror film and made light of them while using them to scare the characters in the *Scream* franchise. The idea of not taking fear seriously, while also scaring the crap out of the audience, is a contemporary twist on the tried and true genre. However, the use of comedy in horror is not new—the comedy duo of Abbot and Costello starred in *Abbott & Costello Meet Frankenstein* in 1948.

The Sixth Sense played on the fear of ghosts while offering the idea that ghosts are not out to harm people—they just need the help of human beings so they can continue on their journey to the afterlife.

From these examples, it's clear that it's important to create a high-concept premise for your horror screenplay if you want to catch the attention of the industry within a genre that tends to repeat itself.

The fairytale Hansel and Gretel's basic premise is this:

> *At the demand of their stepmother, two children are left in the woods by their father to fend for themselves. They must fight for their lives after being taken in by a witch whose goal is to eat them.*

My updated premise is:

> *At the demand of their stepmother, two wealthy teens are lost in the forest during a family vacation. They must fight for their lives after coming upon an isolated condo whose owner is a vampire cult leader bent on drinking their blood.*

Choose a Foreboding Title

The title of your horror-fantasy screenplay should hint at the horror to come. I've decided to write in the sub-genre of neo-horror-thriller, and my title is *Snare*.

Choose Your Chilling Theme

At the core of writing successful horror is reaching inside the audience's collective inner fears and stimulating the subconscious fears of the viewers.

What constitutes a good scare boils down to themes of the supernatural, psychological or biological that develop against a backdrop of increasing tension. Horror films allow you to tackle upsetting issues from the safe distance of allegory. This permits a safe confrontation of real fears disguised in conquerable, metaphorical form. Stephen King, the world's bestselling horror writer, believes that Mary Shelley's *Frankenstein*, Robert Louis Stevenson's *Dr. Jekyll and Mr. Hyde* and Bram Stoker's *Dracula* lay the foundation for all scary stories. These three books showcase three fundamental horror types: man-made, self-made and back-from-the-dead monsters.[12]

Often, horror themes embrace the abuse of power in society and the distrust of government and other important institutions. An excellent example is the film *28 Days Later* . . . where a powerful virus is unleashed from a British research facility, leaving survivors to fight each other for the little remaining food and water.

"I think a function of horror films is to question what we are, and what we fear makes us what we are . . . In America we know there is controversy about Guantanamo Bay and Abu Ghraib. And we have genre movies like *Saw* and *Hostel* right now—but torture and abuse was not a sub-genre that existed before," comments Christopher Gans, the French director of *The Brotherhood of the Wolf* (2001) and *Silent Hill* (2006).[13]

Film theorists and psychologists say that horror films explore the monster inside of all of us; so much so, in fact, that many horror films feature a mental-health expert as a character, primarily a psychiatrist. This character appears to be present in horror stories to explain for the audience why the horror exists in the context of the story. They are the primary source in "tell" scenes.

There's also a fascination with sexuality in horror films. In her book *Men, Women and Chainsaws: Gender in the Modern Horror Films*, Carol Clover explores the idea of ambiguous gender identity, of male killers with feminine attributes and of female heroes with masculine attributes.[14] On a more practical level, Clover talks about the concept of the "final girl," which refers to the last person alive—usually a woman—to confront the killer, ostensibly the one left to tell the story. The "final girl" character can be found in *Halloween, Friday the 13th, I Know What You Did Last Summer, The Texas Chainsaw Massacre* and *Resident Evil*, just to name a few.

For the writer, it all comes down to exploring themes that exist around contemporary society's biggest fears—usually taboo subjects—by finding a way to personify these fears for the audience. It's for good reason that feminism has become a lightning rod theme in horror genre because how the media portrays women is a hot topic. Because American culture perceives women as weaker than men, it is convenient to use them as victims in horror films. However, there's a trend away from such portrayals and, in fact, it's more popular to portray women as the stronger characters in horror films.

Horror film storytelling often uses religion because monsters exist in the Bible. Sometimes religion is the source of a monster's downfall in films. For example, the sight of the holy cross causes physical pain for Dracula and burns his flesh when touched. Frankenstein represents man's pursuit to play God by creating life outside the womb; outraged citizens defeat the mad scientist because of their faith. Sometimes the hero uses Bible scriptures as a weapon against evil, such as in the film *The Exorcist* (1973).

So, while the themes used in horror may seem limited, they are, in fact, a great source from which to draw stories. Each new generation faces its own collection of fears, which have often been handed to them by the previous generation. Look to life around you to draw ideas for your horror screenplay.

Snare's Theme

My story takes advantage of the contemporary fear of terrorism and torture, using humans as the "monsters." To make the script more appealing to a youthful audience, I'll explore the lack of personal responsibility in the children of the wealthy (the fear-of-self-annihilation element) and the use of drugs and alcohol to escape reality. My primary metaphor is: despite the abundance of personal electronic devices (cell phones, the Internet), there's little communication between parents and children, and too many parents—especially those of excellent financial means—seem to be more concerned with themselves in the here-and-now than the future of society their children must create.

Horror-Fantasy Storytelling: Structure & Plot

"I don't think it's an accident that it's always average kids who come to these movies," says Wes Craven. "They're wondering, 'Just how violent is this adult world?'"[15] While the "slasher" brand of horror reigns supreme in contemporary marketplace, it's still important to understand that gore and guts aren't the only ingredients that make this genre successful.

In this spirit, here are a few basic guidelines:

- Horror should scare the audience.
- Keep blood to a minimum because, more often than not, what is *not* seen is scarier than what *is* seen.
- Keep the pace slow and exploit the "in-between-terror" concept (which I will explain later in this chapter).
- Break taboos—in *Psycho* (1960), the main character dies a horrible death thirty minutes into the movie.
- Stick with human villains, in effect creating *real* monsters.
- Give the audience a protagonist they care about.
- Limit the number of settings and locations, because horror films tend to be low budget.
- Pare down the use of dialogue so your film will appeal to foreign audiences.
- Work hard not to be too derivative—unless that's the point, as in a parody.

The psychology of horror storytelling embraces the notion of fear of self-annihilation: that people—the audience—hide in false security of anonymity and individual isolation makes us vulnerable to physical and mental forces. Horror stories force us to walk a tightrope between two kinds of self-annihilation: (1) the eclipse of the self, which hides in the false security of anonymity, and (2) the dreaded individual forces, which gang up on our weakness.[16]

Translation: it's your job as the writer to awaken viewers from their personal nightmare and force them to live through it with their eyes wide open.

Like comedy, the horror genre is audience-interactive; therefore, the screenwriter must constantly consider what the audience is feeling at every moment, because each member brings a set of expectations and assumption to the genre.[17]

Film critics and film academicians generally see the slasher brand of the horror genre—also known as neo-horror—as misogynistic and a revolt against feminism; the film *Halloween* (1978) is often considered the beginning of this sub-genre. Use of point-of-view is an important approach to writing the slasher, given that the audience sees the victims through the killer's eyes. In effect, the audience takes part in the killing. Another staple of the slasher is the teenage victim.

To pull the audience to the edge of their collective seat, not only should you throw the protagonist into the unknown, but you also must make sure he or she can't control his or her life. Examples are the characters in *Final Destination* franchise (2000–2006) or, classically, Rosemary in *Rosemary's Baby* (1968).[18]

Dan O'Bannon, screenwriter of such box office successes as *Alien* (1979) and *Total Recall* (1990), wrote the horror spoof of George Romero's *Night of the Living Dead* (1968), called *Return of the Living Dead* (1985). O'Bannon says that the key to creating a scary horror film is to use what he calls the "terror-in-between" concept: the scariness comes from the slow times that take place in between shots of the monster jumping out of the shadows.[19]

By comparison, the audience never sees the monsters in *Invasion of the Body Snatchers* (1956 & 1978), leaving the horror of who or what has masterminded these attacks to the imagination (and inner fears) of the audience.

Horror story structure, like all popular genres, is formulaic, so these plots are fairly worn. That's why it's extremely important to create fear, so the audience can get caught up in what's happening to the characters—especially the protagonist—and not care so much about knowing what's going to happen next. The audience's participation in the fear is the equivalent of a roller-coaster ride: we ride it repeatedly to relive the terrifying feeling.

Much horror embraces mythological monsters, such as Dracula, Frankenstein, the Wolfman or variations thereof. Therefore, the horror story must be structured to properly set up the folklore—that's Act One—so the audience will understand what is going on. The middle of the story—that's Act Two—must show the power of the monster through a series of escalating confrontations with the characters, especially the hero. Often there's a trail of victims, slowly creating a situation where the protagonist is the only one left standing. And probably the most important thing to remember about the structure of a horror screenplay is that in the end—that's Act Three—you must leave the audience with the feeling that the "monster," though defeated, could still be out there waiting to strike again.

Based on the fairytale Hansel and Gretel, here's the basic story for *Snare* (you'll recognize the opening sequence)

David (eighteen) sits up screaming. *Elizabeth Babncock* moves down a dark hallway lined with dull gray steel doors. Behind her is someone pushing a hemodialysis machine. She goes into David's chamber with the machine, snaps fake vampire fangs into her mouth. As David screams, *Erin* and *Scarlet* dread their turn. *Jackson* (eighteen) waits in defiant anticipation.

In Salt Lake City, Utah are *Hanley Huntington*, his girlfriend, *Emma Johnston*, and his perpetually angry fraternal twin sister, *Gretchen Huntington* (obviously spoiled rotten by her father, *Bradford "Biff" Huntington*). They practically exude wealth. It's clear that Bradford's relationship with his wife, *Isabella*, is troubled, and that the marriage is headed for divorce.

Brad and Isabella—arguing the whole time—take their son, his girlfriend Emma and their daughter Gretchen on their annual family vacation. But this time it's not the regular spot; Isabella has insisted they go hunting and fishing at a lodge in Eagle Mountain, Utah. During a hike in the mountain forest, an unseen group of men abducts the teens. Back at the lodge, Brad gets a call from the kidnappers demanding a large ransom. Brad wants to call the FBI but Isabella insists they follow the kidnapper's demands or the teens will be killed—"Don't you watch TV?" They argue over what to do.

Hanley, Gretchen and Emma manage to escape from their captors and run off into the thick forest. They come upon a luxurious private vacation condominium shrouded by trees in the middle of nowhere. They go there to call for help. The woman who answers the door is none other than Elizabeth. The teens unwittingly enter her lair, and it's clear that the men who kidnapped them—watching from an unseen perch nearby—allowed the teens to escape.

Hanley, Gretchen and Emma are charmed into visiting the bowels of the contemporarily designed and furnished condo where Elizabeth keeps her kidnapped victims. Once there, the new "guests" are hooked up to the hemodialysis machine along with the other captives, and their blood is drawn to provide the elixir for Elizabeth's cult ritual. Hanley, Gretchen and Emma are terrified.

Whenever they can, the teens talk, and soon Hanley realizes that all of them have the same background—they're children of wealthy divorced parents who have been abducted at various ages over the last ten years. Hanley convinces *David*—who seems to have lost his will to fight because he's been there since he was eight years old—that they should formulate an escape plan. Hanley, Gretchen and Emma realize they aren't alone as a cult of vampire worshippers reveals themselves in various frightening ways. Then, during a ritual ceremony, *Erin* is sacrificed. Her death shocks the remaining teens, who now realize they must find a way to escape the same destiny.

Hanley, Gretchen, Emma, David and Jackson manage to escape—along the way finding the remains of many other victims—and flee into the thick forest surrounding the condo. They quickly become hopelessly lost. David and Gretchen commiserate and realize they're attracted to each other—Gretchen has found someone more flawed than herself. They're found by a team of forest rangers, but soon realize their rescuers are members of the vampire cult they're trying to escape. They've walked right back into the clutches of their captors! Hanley, Gretchen, Emma, David and Jackson are taken back to the condo. Gretchen's bad attitude gets her killed by Elizabeth. Hanley, Emma, David and Jackson are now mad as hell and more determined than ever to escape their nightmare.

They begin to lose all hope when they learn that they're presumed dead; Elizabeth has the newspaper stories to prove it. The more Hanley, David and Jackson talk, the more they realize they all have one person in common: Isabella. They now realize that surviving this ordeal would be impossible.

Meanwhile, Isabella learns Hanley is still alive and it's revealed that she's a serial husband-killer who works with Elizabeth to get rid of the husbands' children. The condo is their snare. When she learns that Hanley, David and Jackson are still alive, she realizes she could very well get caught. Using the fake forest rangers, she convinces Brad to join them to retrieve Hanley and Gretchen—failing to tell him that his daughter is dead. Her secret plan is to kill them all, including Elizabeth. Meanwhile, Hanley, David and Jackson try to escape but fail. David dies in the process. The vampire cult now plans to finish off the two remaining boys in an imperative cult ceremony that must take place during a particular alignment of the planets that only occurs once every five hundred years.

Fighting past the fake forest rangers, Brad gets Hanley and Jackson out of their dungeon chambers. They must defend themselves against the vampire imposters, who are now in full regalia and intend to kill them once and for all. They do escape, but Elizabeth seems to have disappeared into thin air.

Back at the hunting and fishing lodge, Elizabeth confronts Isabella and reveals she's not just a cult leader but also a real vampire! This is Elizabeth's only chance to become fully human, or she's destined to be the living dead for five hundred more years. She kills Isabella with a bite to the neck and sucks her dry of blood. Elizabeth completes her ritual and is now fully human again.

Later . . . Isabella rises from a coffin at night: she's now a vampire and mad as hell at how she got there.

Create a Love-Story Subplot

The love stories are Hanley Huntington's sexual relationship with his girl-friend, Emma Johnston, and his sibling rivalry with his fraternal twin sister, Gretchen Huntington, who seems to be angry at the world for everything. Integral to these relationships is their father, Bradford Huntington. There's also a short-lived love story between Gretchen and David to help reveal more dimensions in her character. It is through these relationships that I will explore the family themes in the screenplay.

The Horror-Fantasy Writing Style

It's crucial to write a screenplay that captures a sense of the horror in which the characters are involved. The reader is the first audience, and you must draw the reader into the premise and make him or her participate in the story's horror. Below are some examples of how successful horror screenwriter's do that.

Wes Craven, considered one of the masters of horror, creates a frightening introduction to the villain in the screenplay for *Nightmare on Elm Street* (1984):

```
TINA opens her mouth to scream but only a dry, yel-
low dust pours out. And at that precise moment a
huge shadowy MAN with a grimy red and yellow
sweater and a weird hat pulled over his scarred
face lunges at her. And it's his fingers that are
tipped with the long blades of steel, glinting in
the boney light and giving the hulk the look of an
otherworldly predator.
```

Here's Clark Gregg's opening action-description in his screenplay *What Lies Beneath* (2000) to set up the audience for a horror-thriller:

Moving through a murky haze. Dark blues and greens, shafts of prism purple. A pale shard appears in the distance. Gliding closer, a group of tiny fish dart before the camera.

We're UNDERWATER. Arriving at the form, it finally sharpens into focus. It's a WOMAN'S BODY submerged in dark water, arms floating lazily at her side. The face is obscured by flowing hair. All that is visible is a pair of COLD, STARING GREEN EYES, which blink closed . . .

David S. Goyer vividly describes the death of a vampire in his screenplay for *Blade II* (2002):

BA-BANG! A silver-tipped bullet punches through T-Bag's chest. He turns to ash even as his fellow vamps dash through the disintegrating cloud that used to be his body. The embers melt the snow where they land.

Here's a short sample horror sequence I've written:

INT. VAMPIRE LUCIFER'S LAIR - UNDERGROUND

Nick lies, bloodied, sweating profusely. But he's alive.

Vampire Lucifer looms over Nick.

Nick finds the strength to draw his gun as Vampire Lucifer kneels beside him.

Nick FIRES—BOOM! BOOM! BOOM! BOOM! BOOM! It's empty!

The hot lead does not faze Vampire Lucifer.

Nick's expression says "Now what?"

Vampire Lucifer simply slips one of his needle-like claws into the vein in Nick's arm.

A hot venom sizzles into his body, smoke emanating, Nick is turning purple—

Nick SCREAMS bloody murder!

INT. TUNNEL - UNDERGROUND

The scream catches Spencer's ear.

> SPENCER
> Nick! Nick!

Another SCREAM from Nick!

> SPENCER
> Oh, God—Nick!

INT. VAMPIRE LUCIFER'S LAIR - UNDERGROUND

Nick, now paralyzed, looks into the face of Vampire
Lucifer . . . his voice raspy:

> VAMPIRE LUCIFER
> I prefer my meals to be nice and
> warm. Not hot. But warm.

Vampire Lucifer leans forward . . . his lips part,
revealing teeth like needles.

> VAMPIRE LUCIFER
> You're going to hell.

He sinks his needle-like teeth into Nick's neck.

Nick can't move, can't scream, can only die . . .

INT. TUNNEL - UNDERGROUND

Spencer is on the move, he finds himself back near
where they first entered the tunnel. He sees—

Nick's body: it has been reduced to pale skin over
bones.

Spencer turns, only to face:

Vampire Lucifer. Eyes bloodshot. Needle-like
teeth dripping Nick's blood. Needle claws dripping crimson.

> VAMPIRE LUCIFER
> Time for a little dessert?

Vampire Lucifer's claws puncture Spencer's flesh in
a flash, immobilizing him.

The hot venom starts its trek but—

> BURKE
> Hey, leave him alone!

Vampire Lucifer turns to see Burke, shaky but alive.
Burke slips out what he put in his pocket at the SUV:

A SILVER SPIKE WITH THE HOLY CROSS WELDED TO IT.

He HURLS IT at Vampire Lucifer like a dagger! It hits him—

Right in the heart!

Spencer's relieved of the needle claws, slams his own hand into the Silver Spike, ramming it deeper.

Vampire Lucifer simply vaporizes.

Burke smiles and falls to the ground.

Spencer goes to him.

Burke looks at Spencer.

> BURKE
> Hey, I'm sorry I gave you so much grief, man. But we got that son of a bitch, man. Didn't we?

> SPENCER
> Yeah. We did. Hold on. I'm going to get you out of here. You're going to be okay, Burke.

But it's too late. Burke's eyes close. He's gone.

Figure 5.2 *Writers Guild of America's Greatest Horror-Fantasy Screenplays*[20]

The Sixth Sense, written by M. Night Shyamalan

Horror-Fantasy & Television

The first decade of the twenty-first century has seen a plethora of horror on the small screen, perhaps because of the popularity of horror feature films. Or perhaps it's the proliferation of different distribution outlets that's spurring the exploitation of niche audiences. Of particular interest is the creation of horror series specifically for the Internet.

Horror-Fantasy on TV

Surveying the history of television horror series, only one hit the airway in the 1950s—*Alcoa Presents: One Step Beyond* (1959–1961).

The 1960s only aired one as well—*Dark Shadows* (1966–1971).

For reasons unknown, television viewers missed out on horror in the 1970s.

The 1980s saw *Tales of the Darkside* (1984–1988, remade in 1991) and the remake of *The Twilight Zone* (1985–1989).

The 1990s witnessed what might be considered a golden age for horror TV with *Tales of the Crypt* (1989–1996), *Dracula: The Series* (1990), *The X-Files* (1993–2002), *Millenni* (1996–1999), *Poltergeist: The Legacy* (1996–1999), *Buffy the Vampire Slayer* (1997–2003), *Charmed* (1998–2006) and Angel (1999–2004).

The twenty-first century so far has bought to the airways *Dead Zone* (2002–present), *Carnivàle* (2003–2005), *Night Stalker* (2005), *Medium* (2005–present), *Ghost Whisperer* (2005–present) and *Blade: The Series* (2006).

Your Assignment

Just like in a horror movie, the opening stanza to Edgar Allan Poe's "The Raven" sets the tone for the entire poem:

> *Once upon a midnight dreary, while I pondered, weak and weary,*
>
> *Over many a quaint and curious volume of forgotten lore,*
>
> *While I nodded, nearly napping, suddenly there came a tapping,*
>
> *As of some one gently rapping, rapping at my chamber door.*
>
> *"'Tis some visitor," I muttered, "tapping at my chamber door—*
>
> *Only this, and nothing more."*

Poe is certainly a master of horror. Take a page from his writings and create your own tale of horror. Don't forget, like Poe proved in his works, that the most frightening things in the world exist in our own imagination: fear and self-annihilation. You can get inspiration from greats like Poe and the Brothers Grimm—it's all public domain (and free)—just be sure to update it. Make it your own because originality is a very important ingredient to creating a salable screenplay. However, it's essential to capture the elements expected in the genre by the audience. Use Appendix E: *Horror-Fantasy Worksheet* to guide you in your heavy lifting. I leave you with:

> *And the Raven, never flitting, still is sitting, still is sitting*

On the pallid bust of Pallas just above my chamber door;
And his eyes have all the seeming of a demon's that is dreaming,
And the lamplight o'er him streaming throws his shadow on the floor;
And my soul from out that shadow that lies floating on the floor
Shall be lifted—nevermore!

Now put your butt in the chair and scare the wits out of someone!

Notes

1. Peter Hutchings, *The Horror Film* (Essex, England: Pearson Education Limited, 2004), 3.
2. Stuart M. Kaminsky might be best known for his TV series *The Rockford Files*, which he wrote using Jim Rockford as his fictional hero. However, his Toby Peters mysteries, based in Hollywood, California in the early heyday of motion pictures, are prized by his many mystery-reading fans.
3. Peter Hutchings, *The Horror Film* (Essex, England: Pearson Education Limited, 2004), 1–2.
4. Tim Dirks, "Horror Films," *www.filmsite.org/horrorfilms.html* (accessed March 7, 2006).
5. Steve Neale (ed.), *Genre and Contemporary Hollywood* (London, England: British Film Institute, 2002), 106–107.
6. M. Night Shyamalan also combined horror basics with family drama-thriller elements in *The Village* (2004) and *Lady in the Water* (2006).
7. *Project Greenlight* was a screenplay contest launched by actors Matt Damon and Ben Affleck and producer Chris Moore through their production company LivePlanet, along with Miramax Films. It became a documentary series and first aired on HBO for two seasons, then moved to Bravo for its third and final season.
8. Source: 2005 & 2006 Domestic Grosses, *www.boxofficmojo.com*, as of May 31, 2006.
9. Deborah Netburn, "Why Horror, Why Now?" *www.latimes.com/entertainment/news* (accessed June 1, 2006).

10. Wikipedia, "Hansel and Gretel," *http://en.wikipedia.org/wiki/Hansel_and_Gretel* (accessed June 21, 2007).

11. Source: The Internet Movie Database, *www.imdb.com*.

12. Constance Pittman Lindner, "The Horror Paradox: Why Being Scared Can Feel Good," *www.swedish.org/17032*.cfm (accessed March 10, 2006).

13. Deborah Netburn, "Why Horror, Why Now?" *www.latimes.com/entertainment/news* (accessed June 1, 2006).

14. Peter Hutchings, *The Horror Film* (Essex, England: Pearson Education Limited, 2004), 68.

15. Devin Gordon, "Horror Show," *Newsweek*, April 3, 2006, 61.

16. J.N. Williamson (ed.), *How to Write Tales of Horror, Fantasy & Science Fiction* (Cincinnati, OH: Writer's Digest Books, 1987), 128.

17. Robert Piluso, "Creating the Scream: Writing a Horrible Universe," *www.scriptmag.com/earticles/earticle.php?402* (accessed March 12, 2005).

18. William C. Martell, "Pretty Scary Stuff, Part One," *Scr(i)pt magazine*, September/October 2003, 22.

19. John Scott Lenwinski, "The Terror In-Between," *Creative Screenwriting* magazine, September/October 1998, 19.

20. Source: The Writers Guild of America, West, "The 101 Greatest Screenplays." The list can be found at *www.wga.org*.

6

Comedy-Centered & Romantic Comedy Genres

Make 'Em Laugh

```
EXT. CHICAGO MEAT SLAUGHTER DISTRICT - DAY

The rent-a-wreck truck leaves behind the CATTLE
WREAKING A TRAIL OF DESTRUCTION . . .

INT. RENT-A-WRECK TRUCK - MOVING - DAY

Andrew (30, African American, handsome), Whitney
(28, Caucasian, a cherub) and Danielle (25, bira-
cial: African American and Caucasian, pretty).

                    DANIELLE
          Well, y'all sure are more interesting
          than the last owners. Andy, thanks
          for defending my honor back there.
          That was sweet.

Andrew blushes.

                    ANDREW
          It was nothing.

                    WHITNEY
          It was nothing? It was ten years of
          private karate lessons that defended
          her honor, fo' rizzle.

Danielle grins, gives Whitney a grateful nod.

                    DANIELLE
          Thanks to you, too, Whitney.
```

                    WHITNEY
          (softening)
          Yo, you better recognize.

Whitney takes out a "fun-size" Snickers Bar. Quick
small bites. Fast chewing. Relaxing . . .

                    DANIELLE
          Whitney, I've just got to ask you
          this and please don't take it the
          wrong way . . . Why do you talk like
          you're black?

                    ANDREW
          You don't want to go there.

                    WHITNEY
          Normally, I would tell you to step
          off. But since you are a part of our
          management team, I'm going to answer
          that. I'm fully aware that I'm not
          African American. But I like the
          "flavor," you know what I'm saying? I
          don't mean to offend you two, and
          please don't take it the wrong way,
          but being white all the time is like
          eating vanilla ice cream every day.
          It just gets boring. For me anyway.

Danielle has no response to that.

                    ANDREW
          Now that we've settled that, let's try
          to concentrate on the task at hand.

                    WHITNEY
          Yeah. Let's get paid!

Danielle smiles at Whitney's corny old school hip-
hop pose.

                    DANIELLE
          Well, my naïve and inexperienced bosses,
          I'm afraid we're a long way from that.

                    ANDREW
          What do you mean?

                    DANIELLE
          Hey, I know how to make the dog
          food. But—correct me if I'm wrong—

> distribution, sales and advertising is a part of this equation. And I don't know diddly-squat about any of that.

Whitney gives Andrew a confident look.

>   WHITNEY
> Yo, relax, shawdy. Andy here's all over that, ya dig? Gon' break off a little somethin' somethin' from your plan for us, homie.

>   ANDREW
> I don't have a plan! And stop calling me homie!

Whitney gives Danielle a serious look. In her best Malcolm X voice:

>   WHITNEY
> We been hoodwinked. Mislead. Bamboozled. We didn't land on Doggie Dinners, Doggie Dinners landed on us!

Danielle sees Andrew's irritation, gives Whitney a serious nod:

>   DANIELLE
>   (unsure)
> Word to your brother . . . ?

>   WHITNEY
> That's "mother." Close, it rhymes. Girlfriend, you good to go.

Danielle grins with self-satisfaction.

Off Andrew rolling his eyes . . .

That is a scene from one of my comedy "spec" scripts to set the tone for this chapter. I'm going to explore two sides of film comedy—comedy-centered and romantic comedy—because the film industry develops and markets them as two different genres. However, I must point out that Hollywood studios often market a film as one genre when it's technically another—or a combination of different ones—because their primary goal is to put as many butts into theater seats as possible.

Let's begin with some history.

The Origins of Comedy

While the first comics came from the circus, burlesque, vaudeville or pantomime, the first film studio that emerged to exploit the comedy genre was the Keystone Company. Formed in 1912, this studio quickly became the leading producer of slapstick and comic characters on the silver screen.

Comedy began in film as silent shorts. The action appeared frantic and frenzied, created by the use of a slow camera speed that accelerated in the projector. This technique produced a sense of exaggeration for the audience, which added to the unreality of the situations. The most popular films involved bumbling comedy police officers called the Keystone Cops. The exaggeration allowed the audience to believe situations involving flying pies and bricks, careening vehicles with people holding on for dear life, death-defying crashes and other dangerous-looking stunts.[1] The comic geniuses of early films were Buster Keaton, Harold Lloyd, Laurel and Hardy, the Marx Brothers, W.C. Fields and Mae West.

Films that used lunacy, craziness, eccentricity, ridiculousness and erratic behavior—called *screwball comedies*—dominated from the mid-1930s to the mid-1940s. Then the popular sub-genre of romantic comedy films emerged, and filmmakers Frank Capra, Howard Hawks, Garson Kanin, Preston Sturges, Billy Wilder and George Cukor became the best in this genre. Screwball comedies featured some of the most respected dramatic actors of the time: Katharine Hepburn, Barbara Stanwyck, Claudette Colbert, Jean Arthur, Irene Dunne, Myrna Loy, Ginger Rogers, Cary Grant, William Powell and Carole Lombard.[2]

In the 1950s and 1960s, comedic teams such as Abbott and Costello and Jerry Lewis and Dean Martin (*The Nutty Professor* [1963]) were extremely popular on the big screen. Other 1960s comedy film hits included *The Pink Panther* (1963), *The Graduate* (1967) and *The Odd Couple* (1968).

In the 1970s, Woody Allen (*Annie Hall* [1977] and *Manhattan* [1979]) and Mel Brooks (*Blazing Saddles* and *Young Frankenstein* [both 1974])—moved to the forefront of comedy writer-producer-directors.

In 1980, the Zucker Brothers teamed with Jim Abrahams to lampoon the disaster films from the 1970s with *Airplane!* This spawned parodies of the spy film with *Top Secret!* (1984), crime televisions series with *The Naked Gun* (1988), and military action films with *Hot Shots!* (1991). Filmmaker John Hughes created a very successful series of "coming of age" teen comedies, including *Sixteen Candles* (1984), *The Breakfast Club* (1985), *Pretty in Pink* (1986) and the cult hit *Ferris Bueller's Day Off*

(1986). Hughes' films featured classic rock and roll as well as contemporary music scores, and set a trend for teen comedy films.

In the last decade of the twentieth century, television became a dominant source of comedy talent for film, launching such stars as John Belushi, Steve Martin, Chevy Chase, Eddie Murphy, Dan Aykroyd, Bill Murray, Billy Crystal and Jim Carrey, many of whom leapt to prominence on the innovative late-night sketch comedy series *Saturday Night Live*.

Popular Comedy Sub-Genres

Based on modern film releases, here are the most popular comedy sub-genres:

Romantic comedy: *Fifty First Dates* (2004), *Hitch* (2005), *Wedding Crashers* (2005), *Failure to Launch* (2006) and *Knocked Up* (2007).

Coming of age: *Freaky Friday* (2003), *13 Going on 30* (2004), *Superbad* (2007) and *Hairspray* (2007).

Raunchy: the *American Pie* franchise (1999–2003), the *Deuce Bigelow* movies (1999–2005), *Old School* (2003), *Mean Girls* (2004), *The 40 Year Old Virgin* (2005) and *I Now Pronounce You Chuck & Larry* (2007).

Modern screwball: *Two Weeks Notice* (2002), *Down with Love* (2003), *How to Lose a Guy in 10 Days* (2003) and *Intolerable Cruelty* (2003).

Satire: *Best in Show* (2000), *A Mighty Wind* (2003) and *Thank You for Smoking* (2005).

Parody and spoof: the *Austin Powers* franchise (1997–2000) and the *Scary Movie* franchise (2000–2006).

Dark comedy: *Bad Santa* (2003), *Ladykillers* (2004) and *The Stepford Wives* (2004).

Animation: *Cars* (2006), *Ice Age: The Meltdown* (2006), *Over the Hedge* (2006), *Ratatouille* (2007) and *The Simpsons Movie* (2007).

Figure 6.1 *Top Grossing Comedy Films*[3]

2007

- *Shrek the Third* ($321 million)
- *The Simpsons Movie* ($183 million)
- *Wild Hogs* ($168 million)
- *The Bee Movie* ($123 million)
- *Superbad* ($121 million)

- *Hairspray* ($118 Million)
- *Blades of Glory* ($118 million)
- *Evan Almighty* ($100 million)
- *Meet the Robinsons* ($97 million)

2006

- *Night at the Museum* ($250 million)
- *Cars* ($244 million)
- *Happy Feet* ($198 million)
- *Ice Age: The Meltdown* ($195 million)
- *Over the Hedge* ($155 million)
- *Talladega Nights: The Ballad of Ricky Bobby* ($148 million)
- *Click* ($137 million)
- *Borat* ($128 million)
- *The Devil Wears Prada* ($124 million)
- *The Breakup* ($118 million)

Hollywood's Fascination with Making People Laugh

Let's face it: humor is the most universal language in the world, maybe even the universe (hey, there has to be other life out there!). I'd wager my 401(k) that alien beings on other planets in galaxies far, far away are laughing at all the comedies speeding through space from earth's airways.

Seriously, folks, Hollywood studios make comedy films because they appeal to a broad demographic audience—everyone! I'm not making this up. This has been confirmed by lots of research, with studies like "Favorite Films and Film Genres as a Function of Race, Age, and Gender."[4]

It's a simple formula for the studios: the more feet under the seats and faces in the places (theaters), the more money everybody makes. Then there's DVD rentals and sales (where the *real* money is).

It's pretty simple: funny equals profits.

Choose What to Write

When picking your comedy type, do a gap analysis: look at what hasn't been made for a while within popular sub-genres—there are websites containing past years' box office results—and write a screenplay to fill that gap.

More specifically, you need to come up with a high-concept premise for your comedy screenplay. Two heterosexual firefighters masquerading as a gay couple for government benefits hits the bull's-eye. Two single guys crashing weddings for the sole purpose of having sex hits the nail on the head. A forty-year-old man who's still a virgin slams it home.

You get the drift.

Heavy Lifting & the Fairytales

For the comedy-centered screenplay, I'm using The Three Little Pigs. And for a romantic comedy, I'm using Goldilocks and the Three Bears.

More on both as we proceed.

Comedy Characters & Casting

The movie industry is beginning to rely more and more on stars from television comedies, because these celebrities have the potential to attract large audiences to feature films, thus creating profitable ticket sales at the box office.

So, as a screenwriter looking to create the next hit comedy film, analyze the current stars on the small screen for potential on the silver screen and then write with them in mind. While this is admittedly difficult, look for those television actors with hit series who are appearing in small movie roles. For example, Kevin James from the long-running CBS sitcom *King of Queens* has audiences laughing him up from the small screen, which has also worked on the big screen in such successful films as *Hitch* (2005) and *I Now Pronounce You Chuck & Larry* (2007). Or look for those actors who are standouts in small roles on TV shows. It was a well-educated guess that Steve Carell (*40 Year Old Virgin* [2005] and *Evan Almighty* [2007]) could become a film star after he slowly moved up from a featured bit on the cult television series *The Daily Show*. Comedy actor Jack Black is another example of someone who worked his way up from small bit parts on television to starring roles in feature films.

Screenplays are often optioned or purchased because of the potential roles for upcoming actors. Without a doubt, many of the films that Billy Bob Thornton starred in early in his career would not have gotten out of development if not for his stellar performance in *Sling Blade* (1996). Thornton offered a fresh casting approach for hard-to-market dark comedy films such as *Pushing Tin* (1999).

The old actor's quip "dying is easy but comedy is hard" can't be truer than when it comes to *writing* comedy. Hey, if ain't on the page, it ain't on the screen. So it doesn't hurt to think in fresh ways of the kinds of characters you create in your screenplay. Sometimes actors who are not known for comedy re-invent themselves (and their careers) in comedy films. Robert Stack and Lloyd Bridges re-launched their acting careers with roles in the comedy *Airplane!* Leslie Nielsen did the same in the *Naked Gun* film franchise. And Robert Wagner, known for playing debonair characters early in his career, became a comedy star by portraying Number Two in the *Austin Powers* film franchise.

It also doesn't hurt to imagine big comedy stars in your screenplay, like Will Ferrell, Jim Carrey or Adam Sandler, because each of these actors brings a different and unique quality to a performance. Adam Sandler is different from Woody Allen and Steve Martin from Eddie Murphy. Ideally, you want producers, directors and studio executives to be able to envision a star playing your main character. Also consider casting against type; Robert DeNiro brought his mobster/tough guy persona to such films as *Analyze This* (1999) and *Meet the Parents* (2000) to create hilarious scenes, sequences and sequels to both films.

It's important in comedy to create supporting characters that character actors can play. If executives can imagine involving talent such as Paul Giamatti (*Sideways* [2004]), Jon Lovitz (*The Producers* [2005]) or Eugene Levy (the *American Pie* franchise [1999–2003]), it will definitely boost your screenplay to a more commercially viable one at a studio.

Finally, contrast characters by making them unpredictable allies, such as the classic pairing in *The Odd Couple*. Or put your characters in unfamiliar situations, making them "fish out of water." For example, in *The Game Plan* (2007), a star NFL quarterback suddenly discovers a kid he didn't know he had, or in *The Pacifier* (2005), a tough Navy SEAL gets a new assignment: babysitter.

Choose Your Protagonist

In my update of The Three Little Pigs, I'm not going to have the first two piggies eaten by the wolf. Being eaten by a wolf is not funny. As you've already read in the sample scene at the start of the chapter, the main "little piggy" is *Andrew Brooks*. This character is more of the "straight man" in the trio. I'm using the image of Anthony Anderson (*The Shield* [2002],

Transformers [2007] and the TV series *K-Ville* [2007]). I've chosen him for his comic sense and because he's a believable love match (a lovable teddy-bear type) for his antagonist, a cherub. Here's his thumbnail sketch:

> *Andrew Brooks* (thirty-ish) African American, handsome, could stand to lose a few pounds. Ambitious, he's a Harvard Business School graduate and stockbroker looking to control his destiny by owning his own company. Since he's been around the pet food industry all his life (his father works for the number one dog food company in the world), he engineers a friendly takeover of a dog food company. He's a straight-laced, no-nonsense guy who needs to learn to relax and enjoy life more.

Give Your Protagonist a Strong Goal

Andrew's goal is to buy a pet food manufacturing company, then make it competitive in the marketplace against the giant rival companies.

Choose Your Antagonist

My second "little piggy" is *Whitney*. For her I'm using the image of Drew Barrymore. Obviously, this is an interracial love story (making it a bit risky for purchase, but I'm going for it anyway). Here's a thumbnail sketch:

> *Whitney Metcalfe* (thirty-ish) Caucasian, a cherub, could have been the head cheerleader in high school but has put on a few extra pounds. She's a "clothes hog" and only wears the latest designer fashion. She reeks of a privileged upbringing, and in fact does have a large trust fund. Since she was practically raised by her personal attendant (the politically correct term for *butler*), a stately African American man, she tries way too hard to act "black," in part because she thinks it's cool. She gets her inside scoop on hip hop culture strictly from the media—and it's obvious.

Give Your Antagonist a Strong Goal

Whitney identifies with Andrew's struggle for independence and sees being the co-owner of a pet food company as a way of using her money to break away from her absentee father's influence.

A Key Pivotal Character

My third "little piggy" is *Danielle*. I'm using the image of singer/actor Beyoncé Knowles (*Austin Powers* [2002] and *Dreamgirls* [2006]). Here's a thumbnail sketch:

> *Danielle Thomas* (mid-twenties) biracial: African American-Caucasian, with a slammin' body. She's not long out of graduate business school. Born and raised in Atlanta, Georgia, she has a distinct southern drawl. Though she can be prim and proper, she has a great sense of humor and a fun side.

Choose Your Villain

The "wolf" in my story is *McPhee*, a vice president in the biggest dog food manufacturing corporation in the world. I'm using the image of Ray Liotta because of his menacing onscreen presence and because the more serious my villain is in this comedy, the funnier he'll play against the other characters. Here's a thumbnail sketch:

> *John McPhee* (fifty-ish) a mean SOB who will do whatever it takes to win. He's tough and can back it up. He's Vice President of Special Corporate Relations, which is a euphemism for "the muscle." He's feared in the company because no one knows his real background; rumor has it he was a covert operator for the CIA but he insists he wasn't . . . although, if he was, he couldn't admit it anyway.

Develop Your Comedy Premise

Successful comedies, more often than not, utilize a high-concept premise. In addition, many of these high-concept comedy premises challenge accepted morality by being antisocial, and thus often create or offer a higher morality to the audience.

Comedy works best from the ground up, by starting with a premise that is funny in its own right, independent of individual jokes, then creating sequences and scenes that draw from and expand upon the humor built into the story premise.[5]

A basic rule of comedy: put the main character in a particular situation so that the harder he or she tries to get out of it, the more ridiculous things become. This situation, ideally, is high concept. Here are some examples:

- *I Now Pronounce You Chuck & Larry:* two macho heterosexual fire-fighters pretend to be a gay couple.
- *The Pacifier:* a tough Navy SEAL becomes a babysitter.
- *Cars:* the fastest car in the world must repair old roads.
- *The 40 Year Old Virgin:* the title says it all.

Fairytale Premise

Here's the premise for *The Three Little Pigs:*

> *After a wolf blows down the straw and stick houses of two little pigs and eats them, a third little pig builds a brick house to save himself from the same fate.*

Here's my update to this premise:

> *A stockbroker breaks free of his financial and familial frustrations by join-ing forces with two women—a trust fund baby and a plant manager—in a friendly takeover of a dog food company, only to find himself going up against the biggest dog food manufacturing and marketing corporation in the world.*

Choose a Comical Title

My working title is *Gone to the Dogs.*

Choose a Life-Affirming Theme

Academicians who study comedy generally agree that the comic film inevitably says something about the relation of man to society by upholding its values or maintaining that the antisocial behavior of the comic character is superior to society's norms.[6] Man, that's a mouthful. The translation: humor challenges the morals we value as a society by either exalting them or flying in the face of them. It really comes down to challenging the audience's own sensibility as to what is antisocial behavior rather than making strong statements about it. In this way, comedy avoids becoming preachy.

Another way of looking at it is that comedy is built around one kind of implacable inevitability: men are fools.[7] As writers, we have the choice to take this idea literally or figuratively. For example, in the film *Liar Lair* (1997), the theme of "truth" is explored by forcing a lawyer—a profes-sion well known for stretching the truth to its limit—to only tell the truth. This is accomplished by asking the thematic question: "When is it right to lie?" Through the folly of the protagonist, hilariously portrayed by Jim Carey, the audience learns that legal ethics are very different from the principles of raising a son. It's through the foolish behavior of the protagonist that Carey—and the audience—are able to grasp the importance of the differences between legal and family morality. And, of course, the trick is to say this without hitting the audience over the head with it.

The major collision in all successful comedy is a clash of childishness versus social responsibility; this is the underlying force that should drive each sequence in your story.[8] Then, as the writer, you should take theme very seriously in the development of your comic story.

Tragic-comedy, serious comedy and existential comedy reign supreme in the twentieth and twenty-first centuries, in large part because society at large no longer believes in eternal justice, fate or the other metaphysical explanations for human suffering in classical tragedy.[9] Simply stated, American society is getting more cynical with each passing decade. To a large degree, this is the result of the information explosion aided by ubiquitous technology. So, when you look at the box office comedy successes in 2006 and 2007, many of these films explore highly political themes. *Ice Age: The Meltdown* explores the challenge of global warming; *Over the Hedge* explores obesity; *Cars* explores gentrification; and *I Now Pronounce Chuck & Larry* explores gay marriage.

Fairytale Theme

Experts in film studies circles routinely discuss The Three Little Pigs as providing a metaphorical representation of the fears and aspirations of the Great Depression.[10]

The theme of *Gone to the Dogs* updates these fears of poverty from the 1930s by exploring the moral implications of corporate ethics and by asking the question: "How far people will go to achieve success in business?"

Use Comedy Storytelling Concepts

When you look at the types of comedy films that Hollywood makes, you find that the theme of "clashes between childishness and social responsibility" tends to emerge in three main storytelling approaches:

Teenage coming of age. This approach explores the process of learning to comply with established social values. *The American Pie* film franchise looks at the sexuality nexus in contemporary society among teenage boys, teenage girls and adult women. By the way, this is hardly cutting-edge stuff. In fact, the screenwriter of *American Pie* (1999), Adam Herz, explained in an interview that he created the story by asking the question: "Why hasn't anyone done a *Porky's* film lately?"[11]

Body switching. This approach endures because of its visual value. One of the best examples of a successful film using this technique is *Big* (1988), where a boy, frustrated with the travails of puberty, wishes he were a man. A female version, *13 Going on 30*, hit the big screen in 2004. In both films, the theme of adolescents learning adult morality—especially in the areas of love and sex—is explored and mined for laughs.

Role switching. This approach explores morality in a comedic way because it puts the protagonist in the shoes of someone who doesn't share his or her values about the same subject. *Wedding Crashers* (2005) imposes society's morals on a pair of womanizers who have no respect for the holy sanctum of matrimony. In this film (and all the films that use this approach), the protagonist ends up learning that he or she must evolve. In *What Women Want* (2000), a womanizing man actually hears the conscience-voice of women and discovers how to treat them better by learning the values of honesty and commitment. This approach is particularly popular for the sub-genre of romantic comedy, which I'll discuss in detail later in this chapter.

A key element to writing this type of comedy is the use of deception, especially in the "masquerade" plot. Examples of very successful films that use this simple approach are the classic *Tootsie* (1982), *Mrs. Doubtfire* (1993), *The Birdcage* (1996), *Wedding Crashers* (2005) and *I Now Pronounce You Chuck & Larry* (2007). If not a matter of the protagonist impersonating someone he or she is not, the deception can be a simple lie that gets out of hand, so that the more the protagonist wants to come clean with the truth, the harder it becomes to do so.

The Most Popular Comedy Plot Types

The parody: imitates another work in order to ridicule, ironically comment on or poke some affectionate fun at the work itself or the subject of the work. For example, the *Scary Movie* franchise.

The *mocumentary:* a fake documentary. For example, *Best in Show* (2000).

The *romantic comedy:* a funny drama about the power of love (more on that later in this chapter).

Consider combining these plot types to come up with something unique and fresh.

Create a Clear Comic Tone

As a screenwriter, you must first decide what kind of "comic climate" you wish to create in your story, whether it will be satirical, humorous, farcical or ironic.[12] Here are some more definitions from which to work:

Satire: holding up human vices and follies to ridicule and scorn.

Humor: the sense of the ludicrous or absurdly incongruous.

Farce: light drama marked by broadly satirical comedy and an improbable plot.

Irony: incongruity between a situation and the accompanying words or actions, which is understood by the audience but not by the characters.

As you can see from these definitions, the comedy genre humorously exaggerates the situation, the language, the action and the characters. Comedies observe the deficiencies, foibles and frustrations of life, providing merriment and a momentary escape from day-to-day life. They usually have happy endings, although the humor may have a serious or pessimistic side.[13]

Why Do People Laugh?

Why did the chicken cross the road? Well, the answer depends on who's being asked. Malcolm X might say, "The chicken didn't cross the road, the road crossed the chicken." Morpheus (of *The Matrix*) might respond, "Neo, there is no chicken." Lao Tzu (the father of Taoism) might say, "There is no road." This is a familiar joke we've all heard, but comedy in feature films shouldn't depend just on writing jokes.

There are two more concepts important to understanding why people laugh: (1) what's familiar and (2) the unexpected. People laugh because they have certain expectations from familiar situations. And when those expectations *aren't* followed through, you have the opportunity to generate laughter. So, in the "Why did the chicken cross the road" example, we are all familiar with the question because it's a very old joke. For the same reason, we also know the answer: "To get to the other side." What creates the humor is the *unexpected* answer. In this case, character is the relevant ingredient. That's a very important thing to remember when writing feature film comedy: the humor comes primarily from character.

The ironic part of writing comedy is that you must be serious about it. Comedy begins with a dramatic situation. Implicit in drama is conflict, and it's from conflict that humor emerges. Woody Allen and Carol Burnett have been widely quoted as saying, "Comedy is tragedy plus time." That means that, given time, you can find humor in anything, even in the worst things that happen in life.

Another take on that philosophy is "Pain plus truth equals funny."[14] The bottom line is this: if the audience identifies with a character's painful situation, you are offering truth; thus, that pain equates to conflict. Another factor in the success of this technique is to surprise the audience by taking their expectations of the truth (their own experiences) and giving them something entirely different. I'll discuss this technique in more detail later in this chapter.

The Importance of Being Earnest

This is not just the title of an Oscar Wilde stage play, but also a key element to creating comedy: make your characters *earnest*. In other words, your characters must not be in on the joke. The serious, deeply felt moments, more often than not, create the biggest laughs. Just as dramatic tension should increase as a story progresses, comedic predicaments should escalate as you go—a mistake leads to a problem, which leads to a bigger problem, which leads to a life-or-death dilemma.[15]

Create Funny Sequences

Finally, the concept of set-pieces, or sequences, is a very important storytelling technique to use in comedy. As action films use set-pieces to showcase violence, comedy films use set-pieces to showcase hilarity. For example, in *Hitch*, one very funny set-piece involves the protagonist (Will Smith) transporting the antagonist (Eva Mendes) on their first official date—using jet skis as the mode of transportation. As they say, hilarity ensues.

Gone to the Dogs *Story & Plot*

Andrew Brooks works the phone, desperately trying (and failing) to convince a potential investor for his friendly takeover. On his way home, his brand new Mercedes Benz is carjacked in a bump-and-steal scheme. He's left standing in the middle of the street when *Whitney Metcalfe*, driving a candy-apple-red Porsche Carrera, offers him a ride. Then she takes him on wild car chase after his stolen Benz. The carjackers get away and the cops take Andrew and Whitney to jail for speeding and reckless driving.

Whitney pays Andrew a visit at his office concerning insurance issues and overhears Andrew's last hope of a takeover deal evaporate. She offers to invest. He reluctantly agrees. It turns out the dog food company, Doggie Dinners, is on its last legs and near bankruptcy. *John McPhee*, an executive from the largest pet food company in the world, tries to destroy Doggie Dinners' lab equipment to hasten the company's demise. This deed will ultimately be his undoing.

Andrew and Whitney meet the plant manager, *Danielle Thomas*, who realizes she's out of a job. Though jealous of Andrew's attraction to the pretty plant manager, Whitney decides they need her help to succeed in bringing the plant back from the brink of failure.

Low on cash, Andrew, Whitney and Danielle create a plan to score supplies and equipment. First, Whitney and Danielle masquerade as Tulsa businesswomen, with Andrew as the getaway driver. They score raw meat without paying for it, but end up setting off a cattle stampede in the slaughterhouse district.

Next they must score new lab equipment. Andrew masquerades as a pimp and Danielle as his ho. Goal: distract dockworkers as Whitney, playing the role of a government inspector, talks her way into the warehouse. They score the new lab equipment but someone tipped off McPhee. He shows up, armed and dangerous; they narrowly escape with their lives in the ensuing shootout. They now know this is very serious business.

All the danger and adrenaline encourages both Whitney and Danielle to fall for Andrew. But Andrew's more attracted to Danielle, much to Whitney's disappointment.

Fun and games are over. Now they have everything they need, and Doggie Dinners is back in business. They manufacture enough products to go to market, and they plan to introduce a new brand at the tri-state dog show. Doggie Dinners' new formula is a hit with the pooches during competitive feeding tests and creates a stampede, leaving a trail of destruction at the convention center.

Before Andrew, Whitney and Danielle can get their new brand to market, McPhee steals the entire shipment. With the reluctant help of Andrew's father (who works for McPhee's company), Andrew and Whitney engineer a plan to steal back their inventory, only to find it destroyed. Back at their plant, they must start over. Meanwhile, McPhee analyzes the Doggie Dinners formula and duplicates it as his company's new brand. He is trying to put Andrew out of business with his own formula. Andrew and Whitney find out about the plan from Andrew's father and try to foil the production. They fail. In retaliation, McPhee nearly burns down Doggie Dinners' plant.

In the end, McPhee's company gets the new formula to market first but ends up with a disastrous and expensive total product recall because the new product has too much fiber (caused by the damaged lab equipment), which makes dogs fart excessively. Andrew's father finally joins his son to help Doggie Dinners get back on its feet. Andrew realizes it is Whitney he really loves, and Danielle is fine with that.

A Running Gag

I've incorporated a running gag into my script, which is set in motion in the opening sequence: the carjacking of Andrew's brand new Mercedes Benz. A key element of this is the destruction of several new Porsches owned by Whitney. As the story unfolds, at unexpected times, Andrew and Whitney spot the stolen Mercedes, give chase and lose it, again and again, without a scratch, while Whitney destroys a brand new Carrera each time. In the end, Andrew goes to buy a new Benz and discovers the model on the showroom floor is the very one that was stolen from him in the opening of the story! His house key is even hidden under the wheelbase. He drives it off the lot free of charge.

Create a Love Story Subplot

There are two love stories. The first is between Andrew and Whitney, with Danielle as the third wheel. The second is between Andrew and his father and will also explore the theme of corporate ethics.

How to Write Funny: The Golden Rule of Threes

If you write a comedy screenplay, it has to be *funny!* The old adage "If you have to explain comedy you're in trouble" is true, but only up to a point. There's a *craft* to writing comedy. Moreover, the most important skill you must master is writing comedic dialogue.

Use Comedic Dialogue Structure

The structure of funny dialogue uses the rule of threes. To illustrate, I've taken some creative license with a classic Mae West joke:

The straight line: "You told me to come up and see you some time."

The punch line: "Well, big boy, is that a gun in your pocket or are you just happy to see me?"

The follow-up or topper: "You'd better come in before that thing goes off."

Physical comedy fits into the same construction. A look or reaction can act as a straight line, punch line or topper. Alternately, you can use a combination of dialogue and physical expression. Timing (where you place the humor) and rhythm (the length of the lines of dialogue) are also very important.

Create Reversals

It bears repeating: the true essence of comedy embraces conflict (pain) with which the audience can relate (truth). This merger is important because the audience laughs because they are familiar with a situation. Therefore, the art is to take out of context what the audience expects to create an unanticipated result. Call it a *reversal.*

Build Comedy from Situations

To put this technique into practice, utilize the concept called the *area.* Start with something from which to mine humor—an area. Most times it's a situation. Let's say characters have to attend a funeral; therefore, the area is "a funeral." A funeral is not funny in and of itself, but there are ways to extract humor from the characters who attend a funeral. First, make a list of the normal or expected facets of a situation or activity; in this case, a funeral. Then use those as the basis of the humor. For example, mourners cry at funerals—have a character's quiet sob grow into a gut-gripping laugh. Mourners view the reposing corpse—create humor from the way different personalities perceive the actual dead body in the casket; for example, a character might say, "He looks better dead then when he was alive." For visual comedy, put the wrong banner on a funeral wreath: Congratulations! instead of Rest in Peace. Physical comedy includes pratfalls and facial reactions, that is, deadpan or spit-takes. Of course, these verbal and physical elements are most successful when in threes. Some screenplays are more dialogue driven, while others are more physical in terms of their comedy.

Create Interesting & Flawed Characters

The other major component of comedy screenwriting is to incorporate your character's personality, which is essentially comprised of attitudes and values. In this area, it can help to visualize certain actors in the roles in your screenplay. Jack Black, for example, has a manic, irreverent style; he is also very physical in his comedy. Whereas Kelsey Grammar has adopted a verbal, intellectual comedic delivery, most likely because of his long-running television series *Frazier*. Tim Allen has an acerbic tone to his approach. Actors like Jim Carey, Eddie Murphy, Will Ferrell and Adam Sandler all have distinctive styles of comedy that affect the writing of characters.

Use Funny Words

Yes, some words do sound funnier than others. For example, it's funnier for a waiter with a tray of finger snacks to break the tension of a serious moment at a cocktail party by innocently offering "ramacki" rather than "hors d'oeuvres." Or if you're referring to a third-world country, Zimbabwe sounds funnier than Nigeria.

Does Comedy Have Rules?

If it gets a laugh, it works. That's the only real rule. But here are Preston Sturges'[16] "Eleven Rules for Comedy Screenwriting."

1. A pretty girl is better than an ugly one.
2. A leg is better than an arm.
3. A bedroom is better than a living room.

4. An arrival is better than a departure.
5. A birth is better than a death.
6. A chase is better than a chat.
7. A dog is better than a landscape.
8. A kitten is better than a dog.
9. A baby is better than a kitten.
10. A kiss is better than a baby.
11. A pratfall is better than anything.

Comedy Writing Style

You have to make a reader laugh before you can make an audience laugh. Your sense of humor—as well as the characters' sense of humor—must come across *on the page*. Below are some examples of how successful comedy screenwriters do just that.

Adam Herz (*American Pie* [1999]), sets the tone for his protagonist, a teenager obsessed with sex:

> Jim is, uh, physically involved with the scrambled babe. We TILT DOWN to see a small multimedia presentation next to Jim on his bed. Cosmopolitan is open to a sexy model . . . a yearbook is open to the "girls' swim team" section . . . and a dictionary next to Jim, open to the "vagina" listing, accompanied by a big vagina diagram.

Here's a writing sample from *Gone to the Dogs* that demonstrates comedic dialogue style:

> INT. LOBBY - POLICE PRECINCT - NIGHT
>
> A packed house of perps. Andrew and Whitney sit among them, both handcuffed behind their backs.
>
> Whitney glances at America's worst nightmare sitting across from them—an African American Hardened Criminal. He offers her a cold, menacing stare.
>
> WHITNEY
>
> Hi. I was reading in Newsweek that the percentage of black men in jail is very high compared to white men. (more)

WHITNEY (CONT'D)
(nervous beat)
I just want to apologize for slavery.

Andrew offers the Hardened Criminal a terrified, apologetic smile, gives Whitney a harsh "stop it" glare.

WHITNEY
What?

Whitney cuts the Hardened Criminal a grin.

WHITNEY
(continuing)
Did I offend you, sir?

The Hardened Criminal just glares at this folly.

ANDREW
Will you please shut up!

Off the Hardened Criminal's unchanged glare:

COP (O.S.)
Metcalfe! Brooks! Your bails' been
made!

The handcuffs come off.

ANDREW
Excuse me, Officer . . .

Andrew eyes the Cop's name tag with a Dudley Do Right smile:

ANDREW
(continuing)
. . . Williams. Who posted my bail?

COP
Same person who made hers.

INT. PERSONAL PROPERTY DESK — POLICE PRECINCT - NIGHT

Andrew collects his belongings as the policeman picks up another brown envelope, reads aloud:

POLICE OFFICER
Miss Whitney Metcalfe. One diamond
studded President's Rolex.

Whitney collects her belongings as Andrew looks on in surprise.

> POLICE OFFICER
> (continuing)
> One twenty-four-karat-gold diamond
> ring. One Coach designer purse con-
> taining five hundred seven dollars
> and thirty-two cents. One American
> Express platinum card.

Andrew gives Whitney a curious stare.

> WHITNEY
> Never leave home without it. Where's
> the silver dollar?

The Police Officer looks down the list, then shakes the brown envelope — something falls out onto the desk.

Relieved, Whitney grabs the gaudy fake silver dol-lar necklace like it's worth a million bucks. She holds it up, dangling from an obviously cheap, fad-ing, gold-plated chain, smiles.

As they head for the front door, Andrew offers Whitney a business card.

> ANDREW
> Listen, the officer says I need an affi-
> davit from you for my stolen car report.

Whitney takes the card, glances at it wryly, then gives Andrew a flirty smile.

> WHITNEY
> Sure.

They exit into the:

INT. LOBBY - POLICE PRECINCT - NIGHT

GEORGE (65), a distinguished African American but-ler in an expensive suit, stands out among the crowd of handcuffed perpetrators.

He waits patiently as Whitney and Andrew approach.

> WHITNEY
> Thanks for the bail bond, George.

George nods with the air of a well-heeled professional servant. Andrew tries to give him a business card:

> ANDREW
> I'll reimburse you for the bail. Send
> me an invoice.

```
Whitney stops George from taking the card.
                    WHITNEY
        It's okay. This was all my fault.
                    ANDREW
        You think?
Andrew gives Whitney a hard glare, then leaves them.
Whitney presents George with a devilish smile,
looks down at the business card.
```

Figure 6.2   *Writers Guild of America's Greatest Comedy Screenplays*[17]

- *Dr. Strangelove* (screenplay by Stanley Kubrick, Peter George and Terry Southern, based on the novel *Red Alert* by Peter George)
- *Broadcast News* (written by James L. Brooks)
- *Manhattan* (written by Woody Allen and Marshall Brickman)
- *Crimes and Misdemeanors* (written by Woody Allen)
- *Being John Malkovich* (written by Charlie Kaufman)
- *Adaptation* (written by Charlie and Donald Kaufman, based on the book *The Orchid Thief* by Susan Orlean)
- *The Producers* (written by Mel Brooks)
- *Being There* (screenplay by Jerzy Kosinski, inspired by his novel)
- *The Princess Bride* (screenplay by William Goldman, based on his novel)
- *Forrest Gump* (screenplay by Eric Roth, based on the novel by Winston Groom)
- *Hannah and Her Sisters* (written by Woody Allen)

The Romantic Comedy

Now we move to the other main type of comic film: the romantic comedy.

Origins of Romantic Comedy

The basic format of a romantic comedy predates the cinema by centuries, with many of William Shakespeare's plays, such as *Much Ado About*

Nothing and *A Midsummer Night's Dream*, falling squarely within the bounds of the romantic comedy.[18]

With the technology of sound on film growing in popularity in the late 1920s (*The Jazz Singer* was the most popular movie to hit the screen in 1929), "talkies" evolved in the 1930s to a point where dialogue could be edited with relative ease. This helped to spawn dialogue-driven films on the big screen. As a result, the romantic comedy—as a sub-genre of comedy—began to flourish in the 1940s. Supernatural romantic comedies like *Here Comes Mr. Jordan* (1941), *Heaven Can Wait* (1943), *Blithe Spirit* (1945, UK) and *The Ghost and Mrs. Muir* (1947) were the big hits of the time.

When TV sitcoms became popular in the 1950s, fewer comedies hit the big screen. Those that did were usually courtship romantic comedies, such as the sex comedy *Pillow Talk* (1959). Other memorable romantic comedies of the 1950s include *Born Yesterday* (1950), *Father of the Bride* (1950), *Harvey* (1950) and *Singin' in the Rain* (1952). Sex hit the silver screen in a racy way (well, as racy as it could be in the 1950s) with Marilyn Monroe at her prime in *The Seven Year Itch* (1955).

The 1960s and 1970s were not especially good times for the romantic comedy. There were some standouts, like *The Graduate* (1967), *The Goodbye Girl* (1977), *Annie Hall* (1977) and—probably one of Warren Beatty's best films—*Heaven Can Wait* (1978) (a remake of *Here Comes Mr. Jordan* [1941]).

As the twentieth century moved through its final two decades, romantic comedies made a strong comeback, with such popular films as *Mystic Pizza* (1988), *Say Anything . . .* (1989), *When Harry Met Sally . . .* (1989), *Pretty Woman* (1990), *Groundhog Day* (1993), *Sleepless in Seattle* (1993), *Four Weddings and a Funeral* (1994), *As Good as It Gets* (1997), *Shakespeare in Love* (1998), *You've Got Mail* (1998), *Notting Hill* (1999), *What Women Want* (2000) and *My Big Fat Greek Wedding* (2002).

Popular Romantic Comedy Sub-Genres

Romantic comedy, though a sub-genre of comedy, can literally cross over to every other popular genre. However, historically, three plot types have proven to be durable:[19]

The **ensemble**: *My Big Fat Greek Wedding* (2002), *Love Actually* (2003) and *Hitch* (2005).

The **marriage**: *Sweet Home Alabama* (2002) and *Just Married* (2003).

The **love triangle**: the *Bridgette Jones* franchise (2001–2004), *Something's Gotta Give* (2003) and *Along Came Polly* (2004).

"Comedy with romance" increasingly overlaps classic romantic comedy and continues to grow in popularity. I like to call this hybrid *romantic comedy lite*. I believe this trend is occurring because star-driven films are of paramount importance to studios' marketing efforts. Therefore, I'm suggesting adding a sub-sub-genre to this list which could be considered a throwback to early romantic comedies—the masquerade. Here are some examples:

- *I Now Pronounce You Chuck & Larry* (2007)—the co-protagonists pretend to be a gay couple in order to receive family benefits.
- *Failure to Launch* (2006)—the antagonist pretends to date a man whose parents want him to grow up and move out of their house.
- *Hitch* (2005)—a love doctor works in anonymity to help men and woman hook up with the one they love.
- *Wedding Crashers* (2005)—two best buddies pretend to be relatives of the bride or groom in order to have sex with women at the party.
- *Bringing Down the House* (2003)—a woman on the run from the law pretends to be a lawyer's housekeeper in order to clear her name.
- *Maid in Manhattan* (2002)—a hotel maid pretends to be a rich socialite in order to land a man she sees as out of her league.
- *What Women Want* (2000)—a womanizer pretends to work for his new boss, using his newfound power to hear what women are thinking.

The ultimate lesson learned in the masquerade—this is a thematic thing—is always that it's better to be yourself than to pretend to be someone (or something) else. This theme is popular because people face this dilemma every day of their lives, both personally and professionally.

To Be Young, Gifted & in Love

It's important to recognize the popularity of youth in romantic comedy. This category includes both the slacker and teen love stories. With the changing morals of modern society in terms of race and sex, audiences are also embracing young adult ethnic-romantic comedies, especially films with a predominately African American cast. Some examples are *Love Jones* (1997), *The Best Man* (1999), *The Wood* (1999), *Love & Basketball* (2000), *Hav Plenty* (2002) and *Something New* (2006). These films proved that ethnic romance did not have to be sexually exploitive to attract an audience, as was the tone set with *Booty Call* (1997), a film that became the target of criticism from the African American community for its stereotypical portrayal of black men lusting for sex.

If current trends continue, there's potential for the next comedy spin-off to be interracial romantic comedies, even though *Something New*—the story of an African American woman and a white man who fall in love—was not a huge financial success. However, this trend will more likely see African Americans falling in love with Asians or Hispanics, since television programs are pioneering these types of couplings, as can be seen in the ABC network hit series *Grey's Anatomy*, which featured for the first three seasons a male African American surgeon coupled with a female Asian American resident doctor.

Hollywood's Fascination with Romantic Comedy

The romantic comedy is an enduring sub-genre for the studios because audiences love to experience the fantasy of the guy wooing the girl or the girl landing the guy. Women in particular seem to be more attracted to the romantic comedy because, well, there's *romance*—not something that seems to be big with guys in general when it comes to movies, or, a lot of times, in real life. Also, the romantic comedy is an ideal vehicle for female stars who continually face a paucity of interesting roles to play on the big screen. As a screenwriter, this genre affords you (and the studios) the opportunity to attract popular female actors to your project. In the end, this puts big bucks in company coffers. But the most important step for you as the screenwriter is to sell a screenplay to Hollywood producers.

Figure 6.3   *Top Box Office Romantic Comedy & Comedy with Romance Films*[20]

2007
- *Knocked Up* ($148 million)
- *I Now Pronounce You Chuck & Larry* ($119 million)

- *Norbit* ($95 million)
- *Music and Lyrics* ($50 million)
- *License to Wed* (43 million)

2006

- *The Breakup* ($118 million)
- *Failure to Launch* ($88 million)
- *You, Me and Dupree* ($75 million)

2005

- *Wedding Crashers* ($209 million)
- *Hitch* ($179 million)
- *The 40 Year Old Virgin* ($109 million)

2004

- *50 First Dates* ($120 million)
- *Along Came Polly* ($88 million)
- *The Notebook* ($81 million)

2003

- *Bringing Down the House* ($132 million)
- *Something's Gotta Give* ($124 million)
- *How to Lose a Guy in 10 Days* ($105 million)

2002

- *My Big Fat Greek Wedding* ($241 million)
- *Sweet Home Alabama* ($127 million)
- *Mr. Deeds* ($126 million)

2001

- *Bridgette Jones's Diary* ($71 million)
- *The Wedding Planner* ($61 million)
- *Kate & Leopold* ($47 million)

2000

- *What Women Want* ($182 million)
- *Meet the Parents* ($166 million)

Choose What to Write

Conduct a gap analysis of the romantic comedy films released in the past few years. Try to come up with a new sub-genre or sub-sub-genre. As always, it's imperative to come up with a fresh and unique high-concept premise for your romantic comedy. This is really the only way to set yours apart from all others, as this particular sub-genre is rigid in its formula.

Heavy Lifting & the Fairytales

Goldilocks and the Three Bears

The fairytale is about a mischievous little girl who finds an empty house that belongs to three bears. She breaks in and makes herself at home. After damaging their personal property and sampling their cuisine, she tries out each of their beds, then dozes off in one of them. Papa, Mama and Baby Bear return home, find her and eat her.

I'm updating this fairytale to a romantic comedy, so let's get through the homework process.

Create Romantic Comedy Characters

The protagonist in a romantic comedy is the character who most needs love in his or her life, whether he or she is looking for it or not. In many cases, at the start of romantic comedy the protagonist is not interested in love at all. Just look at the protagonists in the list of top box office hits:

- John Beckwith (Owen Wilson) in *Wedding Crashers* only wants to have sex . . . until he meets the girl of his dreams.
- Alex Hitchins (Will Smith) in *Hitch* is not looking for love, but is doing his job matching up other couples.
- Tripp (Matthew McConaughey) in *Failure to Launch* is a thirty-something slacker who doesn't want to leave home but ends up falling in love with the woman his parents hire to lure him out into the real world.

It's important to create a likeable and sympathetic protagonist—the pursuer—regardless of his or her faults as a person. You want the audience to identify with the protagonist's plight in the story, and the best way to accomplish this is to engender the audience to ask, "What would I do if that were me?" Even if the protagonist starts out obnoxious—like Mr. Udall (Jack Nicholson) in *As Good as It Gets* or Nick Marshall (Mel Gibson) in *What Women Want*—he or she must evolve over the course of the story into someone for whom the audience feels empathy and compassion.

The antagonist—the pursued—should also be likable and sympathetic. Why? Because ultimately these two people are going to end up as a couple, and the audience must root for that to happen. The generated conflict between the pursuer and the pursued is not about one being "bad" and the other being "good," but more about them finding a way to be together.

It helps to create an outside influence to this end. *The Bellamy* (named after the late actor Ralph Bellamy) is a nickname for the "other man," and has a dual function in the story: presenting a conceivable alternative to the romantic antagonist, and helping to define who the protagonist is or isn't.[21] This character can be a co-antagonist or even a key pivotal character in the story. I call him or her the *third wheel*.

You can also use pivotal characters to help generate comedy. Create characters that are, well, "characters" in the truest sense, then surround the couple with them for the express purpose of helping or hindering their effort to get together.

It's in this way that you create the two character triangles—one for the mainplot and one for the subplot—in your story. And it's the efforts of these characters that generate the overall storytelling. In romantic comedies, it's very important to create a love triangle for your characters.

Develop the Pursuer

My protagonist, or the pursuer, is *Abby Smythe*. I'm using the image of Renée Zellweger because she can look plain yet attractive at the same time. She has the right on-screen presence as well. Here's the thumbnail sketch:

> *Abby Smythe*, a thirty-something plain-Jane, is a social services manager at a Chicago cancer hospital. Despite having a doctor boyfriend, she's lonely because she's not in love with him. Her only friends are the dying patients for whom she makes arrangements after their passing. She's compassionate, smart and a hopeless romantic who often imagines herself in romantic movies.

Give the Pursuer a Clear Goal

Abby's goal is to land Porter and marry him.

Develop the Pursued

My antagonist, or the pursued, is *Porter Houseman*. I'm using the image of Hugh Grant (playing an American) because he has the right on-screen presence. Here's my thumbnail sketch:

> *Porter Houseman*, a handsome forty-something medical examiner, only has romantic relationships with women with terminal deceases. He's obsessed with death and has a quote for every dying situation. He's running away from his quirky family—who are in the funeral business—in every way possible. He's smart and hates confrontation.

Give the Pursued a Clear Goal

Porter's goal is to stay aloft emotionally by avoiding committing to any relationship that won't end in a predictable death. Eventually, he realizes he can't live without Abby.

Develop the Third Wheel

My co-antagonist (or Bellamy) is *Dr. Thomas J. Smith*. I'm using the image of Ben Stiller because he plays a seriously flawed "suave" character perfectly (think *There's Something About Mary* [1998] or *Night at the Museum* [2006]). Here's a thumbnail sketch:

> *Thomas J. Smith*, a forty-something oncologist, is Abby's boyfriend. He works in the same hospital and doesn't hide his flirtatious ways with the nurses. In one word, he's an ass, though a likeable one. He's only interested in nurturing his relationship with Abby when he thinks he's about to lose her to Porter.

A Key Pivotal Character

Abby needs a best friend and confidant, so I've created nurse *Dani Michaels*. I'm using the image of Queen Latifah (though my character is younger) because her attitude and demeanor are spot on for this character. Here's a thumbnail sketch:

Dani Michaels, a twenty-something, hip nurse with an attitude, is no-nonsense and simply tells it like it is. She'll do anything to help her friend, Abby, land a man. She's ambitious and wise for her young age.

The Three Bears

I have three characters that Abby, my Goldilocks, will have to deal with as consequences for falling in love with Porter:

Bear #1: *Olivia*, Porter's nymphomaniac sister who constantly tries to commit suicide for attention, and then accidentally kills herself.

Bear #2: *Dr. Jackson*, Porter's best friend and a renowned oncologist whose practice helps Porter's terminal girlfriends with their transitions.

Bear #3: *Jake Bromski*, the French Fry King. He is accused of murder and Porter is scheduled to testify against him; Abby will make a deal with him to save Porter's life.

Develop a Romantic Comedy Premise

Because romantic comedy films strive to appeal primarily to the female audience, this sub-genre's nickname is "chick flicks." That's because the underlying plot for nearly every romantic comedy is "boy meets girl, boy loses girl, boy gets girl back and they live happily ever after." This is a simple and important thing to remember—romantic comedy is about two people falling in love but having trouble figuring out how to be together.

In the transition from the twentieth to the twenty-first century, the romantic-comedy premise has had to embrace the high concept as a way of reinventing itself, and thus reinventing the marketing approach for this sub-genre. The premises run the gamut from the sophisticated *No Reservations* (2007) to the wacky *I Now Pronounce You Chuck & Larry*. In fact, this has caused a mutation to the sub-genre *comedy with romance*.

An excellent example of this premise transformation is *Meet the Parents* (2000), which begins with the guy having already gotten the girl, and then having to win over her father. Another example is *Wedding Crashers*, where two buddies—a "love" story in and of itself—go to weddings to pick up women. They find themselves in an emotional dilemma when one falls in love and the other is stalked by a woman he does not love; this nearly breaks up their friendship. In both of these premises, the situation is more important than the characters.

It stands to reason that if you want to break through as a screen-writer writing a romantic comedy, there's much more potential in finding unique ways to spin the tried-and-true elements of the sub-genre. But take care; audiences who go to see romantic comedies have strong expectations, so it's risky to stray too far from the basic formula—not because you can't write a strong screenplay, but because it makes it a tougher sale to agents, managers and studio executives. But that doesn't mean you can't break the rules, it just means you'll need to be prepared for a lot of notes. For example, in 2006, *Breaking Up* succeeded at breaking the rules—that means the film made big money—by marketing itself as an *anti*-romantic comedy. There were a lot of rewrites, with star-producer Vince Vaughn getting involved, and even some re-shoots after audience testing. It helps that the film showcased two very popular stars—one of who had just had a public breakup with Brad Pitt. Now *that's* marketing.

Here's the basic premise to my update of the fairytale:

> *When a lonely woman falls for a handsome but commitment-phobic medical examiner who's only attracted to terminally ill women, she pretends she's dying of cancer in order to land him.*

Pick a Witty Title

I'm calling this screenplay *Love Sick*.

Develop a Romantic Comedy Theme

There's little discussion necessary. The bottom line: all romantic comedies are about the power of love—not money or sex, but how, in the end, love conquers all. The thematic element of deceit plays an important role in the romantic comedy. Deception almost always illustrates for the audience just how desperate the protagonist is to be with the antagonist. A successful romantic comedy doesn't only show us how a couple gets together, but also explores what their getting together means.[22] In the end, romantic comedy is about what each person in the relationship has to lose by getting together.

The Theme-Behind-the-Theme in Love Sick

My basic theme behind the "love conquers all" theme is "be yourself." To expound, it's better to be true to yourself and fail then to succeed under false pretenses. And since this a romantic comedy (albeit a dark one), the power of love is what makes Abby and Porter realize what is important in life through the exploration of death.

Romantic Comedy Storytelling: Structure & Plot

Story revolves around what the pursuer wants, needs and desires (his or her emotions). The events generated by the protagonist's efforts (his or her behavior) to get what he or she wants, needs and desires is the *plot*. So the main narrative (or driving force) for the romantic comedy is very simple: *boy or girl wants and needs love and will do anything to get it.*

You have to think of how the emotional needs and desires of the pursuer can be explored in the context of the story's premise. Here are some major considerations for story development:

Raise the emotional stakes. "What's at stake for the pursuer and the pursued?" Or, better yet, "What do the main characters stand to lose by getting together?" Memorably, in the film *Arthur* (1981), the title character (played by Dudley Moore) has to choose between immense wealth and the girl he loves. In *Mickey Blue Eyes* (1999), Michael (played by Hugh Grant), literally has to choose between the girl he loves and a horrible death at the hands of her mob boss father.

Emphasize internal conflicts. Of course, this means you must find ways to "externalize" these emotions. A good technique is to give qualities of the pursuer's inner conflict to pivotal supporting characters (could be the third wheel), so that when the protagonist deals with these characters, he is, in effect, dealing with his inner conflict.

Develop an emotionally incomplete pursuer. This will fuel his or her pursuit in the story (the plot) to become emotionally complete. Something has prevented or is preventing the pursuer from being able to fall in love, stay in love or keep a relationship healthy—or all of the above. This is backstory for the pursuer.

Let love rule. No matter what, always concentrate the story and plot around the theme of "love conquers all." It's the effects of the pursuer being in love that drives him or her to act on emotion and create the events in the story (the plot).

Learn from mistakes. It's what goes wrong in the pursuer's pursuit of love that he or she learns from the most. These lessons and failures will determines the ultimate outcome of the love story.

. . . *And they lived happily ever after.* Romantic comedies always—let me repeat that—*always* have a happy ending. To be even clearer, the guy and girl *always* end up as a couple in the end. And the protagonist *always* learns something he or she really needs to know in life. For example, the title character in *Hitch*, whose career is helping flawed people find mates, learns that people more often fall in love because of those flaws. Mr. Udall, in *As Good as It Gets*, learns that he can't live happily all by himself, even with his career success. *When Harry Met Sally's* Harry learns that friendship is an important component of a successful love relationship.

This is easy to explain—the mainplot is embodied in a romantic relationship. Period. Don't fight it. Go with it. Romance, romance, romance. It's why people go to see this type of movie.

Use the Romantic Comedy Story/Plot Template

Here's a good way to build your romantic comedy story and plot structure:

Between pages 1 and 10 . . . Pursuer meets Pursued; there's a problem. This first meeting should be entertaining and funny. It should also be clear to the audience that the pursuer and the pursued are going to have problems with each other.

Between pages 11 and 30 . . . problem between Pursuer and Pursued gets worse; Pursuer ends up falling in love with Pursued. This is an important part of the story because you're setting up the hard times ahead for the couple. Characters draw lines in the sand. Friends and family take sides. Introduce a third wheel. The pursuer decides he or she must seek the relationship.

Between pages 31 and 45 . . . Pursuer loses Pursued—and it's Pursuer's own fault. This first "breakup" is dramatically necessary to firmly establish what's at stake for the pursuer by getting together with the pursued; and when all is said and done, the pursuer is unsure if being a couple is really worth it.

Between pages 46 and 60 . . . Pursuer gets Pursued back. It's important by the midpoint of the story for the pursuer and the pursued to become a couple; having overcome several obstacles between them, they're officially in love. You want the audience rooting for them despite all the conflict and outside influences (like the third wheel). Here's a good time to introduce deceit by the pursuer. This deception should backfire later in the story, ideally at the climax in Act Three.

Between pages 61 and 75 . . . Pursuer loses Pursued again—it's Pursuer's doing, and it looks like it's a permanent loss. You want to break up the couple in this sequence (or sequences), not for the deception used to bond them, but for emotional reasons beyond the pursuer's control. This is a big reversal in the story/plot for the pursuer, and he or she (and the audience) should feel that the relationship is over.

Between pages 76 and 90 . . . Pursuer gets Pursued back using deception. Here's where the pursuer must strongly feel that he or she has no choice but to play the deceit card in order to get the pursued back into his or her life.

Between pages 91 and 95 . . . Pursuer commits to Pursued. Now they're back together, and the pursuer is hopelessly in love.

Between pages 96 and the climax . . . Pursuer loses Pursued because of earlier deception—and it looks like forever. The climax of all romantic comedies is the big breakup.

Between the climax and the end . . . Pursued realizes Pursuer's deception was because of love; Pursued forgives Pursuer; they live happily ever after. The couple gets back together because the deception proves the power of love.

The K.I.S.S. Principle

For those who don't know, the K.I.S.S. principle means *Keep It Simple, Stupid.* The bottom line for this genre is to create a *simple* story and plot, but give the characters *complicated emotions.* The best love stories build on the interplay between inner and outer conflict. Most of the time, the external conflict takes place in the work world or the character's public life.

If you look at this template as strictly a formula, then you will probably suppress your creativity. While you don't want to stray too far from the classic elements of the romantic comedy, you do have a lot of flexibility in the structure of the storytelling. Try to capture the spirit of each structural milestone while being creative and seriously funny.

Love Sick *Story & Plot*

Lines from Shakespeare title each major sequence in my romantic comedy screenplay and are included as onscreen graphics:

"Romeo, oh Romeo, wherefore art thou Romeo?" Thankful for the interruption of her date from hell, *Abby* hears a dying patient's last joke. Abby

arranges the woman's funeral and meets *Porter*, a Cook County coroner and the son of the owner of Houseman Mortuary. She's smitten, but quickly learns that he's only attracted to women with terminal diseases. Abby enlists her girlfriend and fellow employee, *Dani*, for help. The plan: fake a cancer diagnosis just to get the romance going. Abby meets Porter's embalmer sister, *Olivia*, who has a penchant for faking suicide for attention—this time with pills.

"To be or not to be, that is the question . . ." The plan starts going downhill fast as Porter insists Abby be treated by his best friend, *Dr. Jackson*, a renowned oncologist, who asks for her medical file. Dani has to fake her file using a closed patient file while *Jake Bromski*, the Polish-Norwegian Mafia's French Fry King, intimidates Porter not to testify in Bromski's murder trial. Abby's on-again, off-again surgeon paramour, *Thomas*, is jealous.

"To die, perchance to dream . . ." Abby discovers that Porter's father is dying. Despite Dani's warning, Abby interferes. Dr. Jackson puts Abby into psychotherapy and her guilt builds. The faked medical file is unknowingly reopened and Abby is now "officially" dying. Now in too deep, Abby uses meds to duplicate the symptoms of chemotherapy—vomiting and weight lost—and shaves her head. The worse Abby looks, the more in love Porter becomes. Still jealous, Thomas pursues Abby with renewed vigor.

"Ah, there's the rub . . ." Porter is smacked around by a massive "wise guy." At the E.R., Abby faints, and unknowingly gets a blood test. Olivia tries to commit suicide, again, by going inside the zoo's lion attraction. Porter makes love to Abby in the morgue. She finally gets the nerve to tell him his father is dying. Thomas crashes the date with a public proposal of marriage.

"The slings and arrows of outrageous fortune . . ." Tiring of the charade, Abby demands new tests so she'll be magically "cured." But Porter's love goes cold. Dr. Jackson gets the E.R. blood tests, realizes Abby's been faking. He decides to use Abby to rescue his best friend from his obsession. Meanwhile, Olivia mistakenly kills herself—she didn't think the gun was loaded. Abby arranges her own kidnapping to force Porter not to testify if Abby is freed. But she still doesn't get him back. Dr. Jackson convinces Abby she must not quit trying to help Porter.

"Oh, what a tangled web we weave . . ." At Porter's father's funeral, the Mafia French Fry King himself appears; he accidentally-on-purpose reveals to Porter that the kidnapping was a setup. Porter is furious. Abby tries to apologize and unwittingly confesses to faking her disease. Abby thought Dr. Jackson had told him, but Porter didn't know. Now Porter wants her out of his life forever.

"Parting is such sweet sorrow . . ." Abby takes a job working with Porter's mother now that her husband is gone. But surprise!—Porter's taking over the mortuary. Abby can't possibly work him, can she? But then Porter offers her co-ownership in the form of a marriage proposal. She doesn't know what to do . . . until all her friends appear, in a bizarre love intervention. Abby accepts Porter's hand, they embrace and kiss. *"All's well that ends well . . ."*

Create a Love Story Subplot

Even though the mainplot in romantic comedy is a love story, you still need a subplot love story in which to explore the story's theme and to develop another dimension of your protagonist. I'm using Abby's relationship with Dani to achieve that in *Love Sick*. This subplot love story is about friendship and loyalty, interwoven with the general theme of "be yourself."

Writing Funny in Romantic Comedy

In romantic comedy, you can create comedy from character, from a situation or from both. The same comedy principles I discussed earlier in this chapter apply to this and other sub-genres. So start with a serious situation or moment and use that as the source of humor by reversing what the audience expects to see or hear in a particular situation.

Remember the tone with which you are writing your romantic comedy: is it farcical, satirical, dark, sophisticated or dramatic? Use the comic set-piece and create memorable scenes, sequences and "house numbers" (scenes with big laughs).

Since you're writing about romance, of course there will be sex involved. However, use the sexual situation as a source of comedy. The big scene where Harry makes love to Sally is hilarious because of its awkwardness. In *Jerry Maguire*, Jerry's first date with Dorothy is cleverly erotic because he's seducing her by putting her clothes back *on*.[23] Be careful with the sex act itself. It's more romantic to create sexual tension than to have the couple actually *have* sex. The most successful romantic comedies avoid the sex act altogether. Indeed, even kissing is treated as a big deal. Of course, if you're writing about how empty the act of sex is without love, then there will probably be a lot of actual sex in your story. But it's best if it's not with the pursuer, so when it does happen (if at all), it has emotional value for the characters and the audience. As I've said before: romance, romance, romance.

Dialogue-Driven Romantic Comedy

Nora Ephron (*When Harry Met Sally*), Woody Allen (*Annie Hall*) and Richard Curtis (*Four Weddings and a Funeral*, *Notting Hill*, *Love Actually*) are some of the best writers of humorous discourse. But don't forget—dialogue must still serve the three major purposes:

1. Develop Character
2. Advance the Story
3. Reveal Conflict

Remember, film is primarily a visual medium, so allow images to help tell the story. Sometimes the audience learns more from a character's actions and reactions than from what he or she actually says. You can accomplish a lot using visual gags. For example, in the opening sequence of *As Good as It Gets*, Mr. Udall does a very despicable—but funny—thing: he puts his neighbor's cute little dog, Verdell, down the apartment building's garbage chute. In *What Women Want*, Nick puts on pantyhose to help him think more like a woman, in order to land a big advertising account.

Romantic Comedy Writing Style

A key thing to remember when writing romantic comedy is that this sub-genre is, at its heart, more a drama than comedy. So the style of the writing should embrace heartfelt conflict and pain. What makes a romantic comedy funny is how serious it is, to the point of incongruity and ridiculousness. The drama becomes funny because the characters don't seem to know when to give up. Here are some examples of writing styles:

The screenwriters of *Wedding Crashers*, Steve Faber and Bob Fiber, introduce one of the primary characters of a comic "running gag":

> This is MARY CLEARY, the grandmother of the bride and the matriarch of the Cleary family. Next, two groomsmen walk the mother of the bride, KATHLEEN-CLEARY, to her seat. She has the glow of someone who has been drinking . . . every day for the last twenty-five years.

The best romantic comedies have funny dialogue, too. Here's a sequence from *Love Sick* where the pursuer, Abby, meets the pursued, Porter:

> INT. CHAPEL - HOUSEMAN MORTUARY - DAY
>
> Abby looks at Sylvia resting peacefully in the casket, her beauty restored in death.
>
> REVEAL — Abby is the sole mourner.
>
> INT. OFFICE - HOUSEMAN MORTUARY - DAY
>
> Porter sits across from:
>
> MR. EMERSON HOUSEMAN (65), a tall, dignified man with a stick up his ass.
>
> Both men are stewing. Finally, Mr. Houseman pushes a form to Porter.
>
> > MR. HOUSEMAN
> > You realize this is absurd.
>
> Porter signs the form.
>
> > PORTER
> > I'll make my own copy.
>
> > MR. HOUSEMAN
> > For your scrapbook, no doubt. These
> > escapades of yours cut into my prof-
> > its. But you don't care since you
> > refuse to be a part of the family
> > business.
>
> Porter stands, tightens his lips and holds in his anger.
>
> > MR. HOUSEMAN
> > (continuing)
> > Not even a thank you. You unapprecia-
> > tive bastard.
> > (more)

>   MR.HOUSEMAN (CONT'D)
>   (beat)
>   You are a bastard, you know. Your
>   mother and I weren't married when you
>   were born!

That does it—

>   PORTER
>   You're a lying son of a bitch!

Mr. Houseman smiles, proud of his power to provoke.

>   MR. HOUSEMAN
>   This is the final freebie, Porter! My
>   business will not continue to finance
>   your deplorable fascination with
>   dying women.

>   PORTER
>   I hate you.

>   MR. HOUSEMAN
>   (mocking)
>   I hate you more.

Porter reaches to open the office door but it
WHACKS him in the face. Blood flows from his nose.

Abby enters, sees what she's done.

>   ABBY
>   Omigod! I'm so sorry.

Abby takes a dainty handkerchief from her purse,
gives it to Porter, then gets faint at the sight of
the blood.

An awkward moment, then Porter hurries off.

>   MR. HOUSEMAN
>   Are you all right, Miss Smythe?

She recovers.

>   ABBY
>   Yes. Uh . . . I just wanted to let you
>   know I'm leaving now.

>   MR. HOUSEMAN
>   But Miss Monroe's mourners have yet
>   to arrive.

>   ABBY
>   I was it. She has no one else.

>   MR. HOUSEMAN
>   I see. Such a shame.

INT. CHAPEL - HOUSEMAN MORTUARY - DAY

Abby returns for her final good-bye. Smiles down at
Sylvia.

>   ABBY
>   You were . . . are . . . such a beautiful
>   spirit, Sylvia. Rest in peace.

>   PORTER
>   One's dying is more the survivor's
>   affair than one's own.

Abby turns as:

Porter approaches, holding the blood-stained han-
kie. Off Sylvia, his face lights up—

>   PORTER
>   (continuing; elegantly)
>   "Either death is a state of nothingness
>   and utter unconsciousness, or, as men
>   say, there is a change and migration of
>   the soul from this world to another.
>   Now if death be of such nature, I say
>   that to die is to gain. For eternity is
>   then only a single night."

Abby is mesmerized.

>   ABBY
>   That's beautiful. Did you write it?

>   PORTER
>   Plato.

He's looking back and forth between Sylvia and Abby as:

>   PORTER
>   (continuing)
>   So pretty. Too bad our paths didn't
>   cross.

Porter gives Abby an ambiguous smile, turns and
leaves.

Abby's not sure who that compliment was for . . .

>   MRS. HOUSEMAN
>   Porter, dear. Call the ambulance.
>   It's Olivia.

Abby's up, heads into the:

INT. PARLOR - HOUSEMAN MORTUARY - DAY

Mrs. Houseman emerges from the basement stairs.
(All are matter-of-fact):

>   PORTER
>   What did she use this time?

>   MRS. HOUSEMAN
>   Pills, I think.

>   PORTER
>   Less messy than slicing her wrists.
>   (to Abby)
>   Her blood doesn't clot well.
>   (to Mrs. Houseman)
>   Conscious?

>   MRS. HOUSEMAN
>   No, dear.

Porter takes out his cell phone, dials 9-1-1.

>   PORTER
>   Same note?

Mrs. Houseman calmly nods "yes." Mr. Houseman enters:

>   MR. HOUSEMAN
>   (more to himself)
>   Must be getting quite dog-eared by now.

>   PORTER
>   (in phone)
>   Hello. There's been a suicide attempt.
>   (beat)
>   Olivia Houseman. Houseman Mortuary.
>   You know the address.

Porter exits.

Abby notices Mr. Houseman standing in the middle of
the waiting room:

Alone. Emotionless. It's odd.

>   MRS. HOUSEMAN
>   So sorry for your lost, Abby dear.

Abby snaps out of her stare.

>   ABBY
>   Oh, thank you.

INT. DESIGNER CLOTHING OUTLET - CHICAGO - DAY

Abby and Dani whip through the sales racks.

                    ABBY
          They were all so, so, blasé.

                    DANI
          Hey, they deal with stiffs every day.

                    ABBY
          You know what I mean.

                    DANI
          Girl, stay the hell out of folks'
          family business. They will turn on
          your ass like a bad hair relaxer.

Abby's about to burst with guilt. Dani notices.

                    DANI
          (continuing)
          You look like the cat who swallowed
          Tweetie Bird.

                    ABBY
          I hit on him.

                    DANI
          What?

                    ABBY
          Seconds after his mother told me his
          fiancée was dying, I actually hit on the
          man. Does that make me a bad person?

                    DANI
          It sure does, but—

Dani gives Abby a high five.

                    DANI
          (continuing)
          You go, girl!

                    ABBY
          But I feel kind of creepy.

                    DANI
          Men say all's fair in love and war, right?

                    ABBY
          Right.

```
                    DANI
          So it's imperative that wo-men use
          our number one weapon . . .

     Dani holds up a sexy dress—

                    DANI
             (continuing)
             Spandex!

     OFF Abby's blush—
```

Figure 6.5 *Writers Guild of America's Greatest Romantic Comedy Screenplays* [24]

- *Annie Hall* (written by Woody Allen and Marshall Brickman)
- *Some Like It Hot* (screenplay by Billy Wilder and I.A.L. Diamond, based on *Fanfare of Love*, a German film written by Robert Thoeren and M. Logan)
- *The Graduate* (screenplay by Calder Willingham and Buck Henry, based on the novel by Charles Webb)
- *The Apartment* (written by Billy Wilder and I.A.L. Diamond)
- *Tootsie* (screenplay by Larry Gelbart and Murry Schisgal, story by Don McGuire and Larry Gelbart)
- *Groundhog Day* (screenplay by Danny Rubin and Harold Ramis, story by Danny Rubin)
- *Shakespeare in Love* (written by Marc Norman and Tom Stoppard)
- *His Girl Friday* (screenplay by Charles Lederer, based on the play *The Front Page* by Ben Hecht and Charles MacArthur)
- *The Philadelphia Story* (screenplay by Donald Ogden Stewart, based on the play by Phillip Barry)
- *When Harry Met Sally . . .* (written by Nora Ephron)
- *The Lady Eve* (screenplay by Preston Sturges, story by Monckton Hoffe)
- *It Happened One Night* (screenplay by Robert Riskin, based on the story *Night Bus* by Samuel Hopkins Adams)
- *Moonstruck* (written by John Patrick Shanley)
- *Jerry Maguire* (written by Cameron Crowe)
- *Harold & Maude* (written by Colin Higgins)

- *Sideways* (screenplay by Alexander Payne and Jim Taylor, based on the novel by Rex Pickett)

Comedy Television Series

Most scripted comedies on television are a half-hour long. However, since the mid-nineties, reality comedy (*The Daily Show*) and improvised comedy (*Curb Your Enthusiasm*) have been growing in popularity on television. This trend will be interesting to watch as more and more outlets on which to present series in general increases. The most obvious place is the World Wide Web, where the advent of video streaming is making it possible to deliver programming to a global *and* highly targeted audience. Comedy is one of the most popular genres being "uploaded" to the Internet because everyone likes to laugh.

Comedy on TV

Here's a sampling—by no means complete—of popular and "classic" scripted series that helped to define television comedy over the decades:[25]

In the 1950s, there was *The Cisco Kid* (1950–1956), *The George Burns and Gracie Allen Show* (1950–1958), *The Jack Benny Program* (1950–1965), *I Love Lucy* (1951–1957)—which pretty much set the standard for situation comedy—*The Adventures of Ozzie & Harriet* (1952–1966), *The Honeymooners* (1952–1978), *Make Room for Daddy* (1953–1965), *Father Knows Best* (1954–1960), *Bachelor Father* (1957–1962), *Leave It to Beaver* (1957–1963), *The Ann Sothern Show* (1958–1961) and *The Donna Reed Show* (1958–1966).

The turbulent 1960s set a surprisingly optimistic tone with series such as *The Andy Griffith Show* (1960–1968), *My Three Sons* (1960–1972), *The Dick Van Dyke Show* (1961–1966), *The Avengers* (1961–1969), *The Lucy Show* (1962–1968), *The Beverly Hillbillies* (1962–1971), *Bewitched* (1964–1972), *I Spy* (1965–1968)—another groundbreaking series that starred an African American man, Bill Cosby—*That Girl* (1966–1971), *The Carol Burnett Show* (1967–1978), the groundbreaking *Julia* (1968–1971)—the first series that starred an educated, middle-class African American woman, Diane Carroll—and *The Brady Bunch* (1969–1974).

The 1970s saw a number of series that featured African American and Hispanic cast members. *The Mary Tyler Moore Show* (1970–1977) set a new standard for mainstream comedy. *All in the Family* (1971–1979) explored a bigot in a starring role. Then there was *M*A*S*H* (1972–1983), *Chico and the Man* (1974–1978)—the first show to star a Latino—*Good Times* (1974–1979), *Barney Miller* (1975–1982), *The Jeffersons* (1975–1985), *Laverne & Shirley* (1976–1983), *Alice* (1976–1985), *Three's Company* (1977–1984), *The Love Boat* (1977–1986), *Taxi* (1978–1983), *The Dukes of Hazzard* (1979–1985), *Benson* (1979–1986) and *The Facts of Life* (1979–1988).

The 1980s saw *Family Ties* (1982–1989), *Newhart* (1982–1990), *Cheers* (1982–1993), *Mama's Family* (1983–1990), *The Cosby Show* (1984–1992)—which set the platinum standard for television comedy—*Night Court* (1984–1992), *The Golden Girls* (1985–1992), *Growing Pains* (1985–1992), *Designing Women* (1986–1993), *A Different World* (1987–1993), *The Wonder Years* (1988–1993), *Roseanne* (1988–1997), *Murphy Brown* (1988–1998), *Doogie Howser, M.D.* (1989–1993), *Coach* (1989–1997), *Family Matters* (1989–1998) and *The Simpsons* (1989–present).

In the 1990s, these series hit the small screen: *Northern Exposure* (1990–1995), *The Fresh Prince of Bel-Air* (1990–1996), *Wings* (1990–1997), *Seinfeld* (1990–1998), *The Larry Sanders Show* (1992–1998), *Mad About You* (1992–1999), *Frasier* (1993–2004), *Friends* (1994–2004), *Arli$$* (1996–2002), *Spin City* (1996–2002), *Everybody Loves Raymond* (1996–2005), *Ally McBeal* (1997–2002), *South Park* (1997–present), *Sex and the City* (1998–2004), *That '70s Show* (1998–2006), *Will & Grace* (1998–2006) and *The King of Queens* (1998–2007).

In the first decade of twenty-first century, audiences were entertained by *Malcolm in the Middle* (2000–2006), *Curb Your Enthusiasm* (2000–present), *The Bernie Mac Show* (2001–2006), *Scrubs* (2001–present), *Chappelle's Show* (2003–present), *Two and a Half Men* (2003–present), *Boston Legal* (2004–present), *Desperate Housewives* (2004–present), *Entourage* (2004–present), *Everybody Hates Chris* (2005–present), *My Name Is Earl* (2005–present), *The Office* (2005–present), *Weeds* (2005–present), *30 Rock* (2006–present) and *Ugly Betty* (2006–present).

Your Assignment

Start with a funny idea. If you can't get a laugh (or at least a smile) from someone when you pitch your idea, it's not ready. Keep working on it until you start getting a laugh.

Start with the familiar and then add the unexpected. The audience (and the reader) laughs when what they expected to happen doesn't.

Give the story heart. The audience is comprised of human beings (well, most of the time; I, too, am disgusted by those people who refuse to turn off their cell phones when the feature attraction begins— *absolutely inhuman!*), and they identify with emotions that parallel their daily lives and relationships.

Make the reader laugh. Use the craft of comedy writing to help you accomplish this. And don't forget that at the heart of comedy is conflict!

Now, get started on writing your comedy screenplay.

NOTES

1. Tom Dirks, "Comedy Films," *www.filmsite.org/comedyfilms2.html* (accessed March 20, 2006).

2. Ibid.

3. Source: *www.boxofficemojo.com/yearly/chart/?yr=2005&p=.html* (accessed July 23, 2007).

4. Joe Antonio, B.A., Stuart Fischoff, Ph.D., Diane Lewis, B.A. "Favorite Films and Film Genres as a Function of Race, Age, and Gender" (paper originally presented at the American Psychological Association Convention, Chicago, August 1997), *Journal of Media Psychology*, vol. 3, no. 1, winter 1998.

5. Evan Smith, "Premise-Driven Comedy: Writing Funny from the Ground Up!" *Creative Screenwriting* magazine #32, July/August 2000, 52.

6. Gerald Mast, *The Comic Mind: Comedy and the Movies*, Second Edition (Chicago and London: The University of Chicago Press, 1973, 1979), 20.

7. Ibid.

8. Stuart Voytilla, "Structuring the Memorable Comic Sequence," *Scr(i)pt* magazine, May/June 2005, 73.

9. Gerald Mast, *The Comic Mind*, 341.

10. Adrian Danks, "Huffing and Puffing about Three Little Pigs," *www.sensesofcinema.com/contents/cteq/03/29/3_little_pigs.html* (accessed June 14, 2008). Note: Disney Studios released a very popular nine-minute animated film of this fairytale in 1933.

11. The 1982 teen comedy *Porky's* spawned two sequels: *Porky's II: The Next Day* (1983) and *Porky's Revenge* (1985).

12. Andrew Horton, *Laughing Out Loud: Writing the Comedy-Centered Screenplay* (Berkeley and Los Angeles: University of California Press, Ltd., 2000), 20.

13. Tom Dirks, "Comedy Films," *www.filmsite.org/comedyfilms2.html* (accessed March 20, 2006).

14. Billy Mernit, *Writing the Romantic Comedy* (New York: HarperCollins, 2000), 152.

15. Evan Smith, "Premise-Driven Comedy: Writing Funny from the Ground Up!" *Creative Screenwriting* magazine #32, July/August 2000, 52.

16. One of Hollywood's legendary directors, Preston Sturges redefined the boundaries and meaning of screen comedy during the early '40s. *The Great McGinty* (1940), a political satire (always considered a risky category for films) astonished everybody by becoming a major hit. Sturges subsequently directed *Christmas in July* (1940), *The Lady Eve* (1941), *Sullivan's Travels* (1941), *The Palm Beach Story* (1942), *Hail the Conquering Hero* (1944) and *The Miracle of Morgan's Creek* (1944), all of which were solid commercial and critical successes.

17. Source: The Writers Guild of America, West, "The 101 Greatest Screenplays." The list can be found at *www.wga.org*.

18. Wikipedia, "Romantic Comedy," *http://en.wikipedia.org/wiki/Romantic_comedy_film* (accessed March 26, 2006).

19. Mernit, *Writing the Romantic Comedy*, 19.

20. 2000 through 2006 Domestic Grosses, *www.boxofficemojo.com/yearly/chart/?yr=2005&p=.htm* (accessed March 28, 2006).

21. Mernit, *Writing the Romantic Comedy*, 66.

22. Ibid., 89.

23. Ibid., 174–175.

24. Source: The Writers Guild of America, West, "The 101 Greatest Screenplays." The list can be found at *www.wga.org*.

25. Source: *www.tv.com*.

7

Marketing Your Finished Popular Genre Screenplay

The Screenplay Is a Product

The last thing a screenwriter wants to think about is selling his or her screenplay. "I'm an artist, why do I need to get involved in the business shenanigans?" you might ask. The answer is simple: a screenplay is not the finished product, but is only the beginning of a long process from conception to consumer. You don't have to get your hands dirty if you don't want to (that's what agents and managers are for), but you certainly need to understand what you're up against and how what you write affects your screenplay's chances of selling and getting produced.

One of the most daunting challenges a screenwriter faces is to successfully run the gauntlet of the film industry *after* writing a screenplay. The odds of you selling your screenplay are long and the chance of it hitting the big screen afterward are even longer. The obvious reality is that more screenplays are optioned and purchased than produced and distributed. (Yes, some produced films are never distributed.) In a way, the idea of selling your screenplay, by necessity, has to be a very persistent dream. Having said this, the process of writing and the process of selling are totally separate—and must stay separate, or you'll drive yourself nuts.

The Writer's Guild of America, West's twenty-four-hour online registration service continues to expand, with more than 70,000 items submitted in 2006.[1] According to the Academy of Motion Picture Arts and Sciences, 307 feature films competed for the Academy Award for Best Picture in 2006 (311 in 2005). While this number is not the total number of films made in that year, it's an excellent gauge of the percentage of screenplays hitting the big screen versus those languishing in the entertainment industry's "development" system.

Unfortunately, the design of the development system isn't necessarily to find excellent screenplays per se, but to screen *out* undesirable material. I know, I know, I hear your groans, but there's a big difference between these two goals. The main job of agencies, production companies and studios is to say no. I'm sorry if this is a negative revelation, but it is the reality. And if you intend to navigate the gauntlet, you must do it with wide open eyes and sharp reflexes.

This chapter provides the basics of the Hollywood system so that you can enter it with some idea of what to expect.

The Four Quadrants

According to Jim Cirile, in his *Creative Screenwriting* "Agent's Hot Sheet" article "Meet the Four Quadrants," *The Incredibles* is a near-perfect four-quadrant movie. He observes that this film appeals to all four main demographic groups—young and old, male and female. In other words, a four-quadrant movie is "everyone's picture." "The larger spec sales and bidding wars come from movies that appeal to a broader audience," says Cirile. Ergo, if you nail the four quadrants, that's where you'll find the big paydays.

Not everyone agrees with this theory. Nevertheless, most experts in the entertainment industry do agree that the search for a screenplay that possess the four quadrants appeal is coveted because it's deceptively difficult to pull off.

From Script to Screen: How Films Get Made

It's important to understand how your creative efforts will be processed and turned into a final product. For the screenwriter, this process seems simple: write the script, find an agent to sell it, collect a sizable paycheck. However, even though what you do as the screenwriter—who actually starts the entire process of marketing—doesn't seem to affect you directly, there are many elements of the business that do affect the creative approach and final outcome of the film.

When you feel your screenplay is ready for industry eyes, the process generally goes something like this:

An agent, manager, attorney or a combination of them "shop" your screenplay. It will be turned down, optioned or purchased.

If someone options your screenplay, generally a producer or director then "shops" your script to the studios and production companies; or, if a producer or director has a production deal at the studio, he or she takes it to executives for consideration.

If a studio purchases your screenplay, the development process begins—lots of rewriting (in fact, chances are you'll get replaced by another writer) while other creative elements are attached to the project, such as a director and actors.

If the screenplay falls out of development, go back to square one. If it's given a green light for production, it moves into the product pipeline. Lots of factors are involved in this step, but two tend to be the most important: the budget and the starring actor's availability.

The screenplay goes into production. Generally, the set during production is the domain of the director, which means the writer doesn't hang out there. During production, "selects" or "select scenes" ship to the marketing department for creating trailers. On major big-budget releases, there are "behind the scenes" documentaries made for publicity and marketing leading up the film's release date. Sometimes the writer participates in on-camera interviews.

Completion of principal photography. The writer might be invited to the "wrap party."

The post-production process begins. This includes editing picture and sound, and creating a music score and soundtrack, since music is a very important element to a film's success. During this time, there may be re-shoots and actors loop dialogue (a process that takes place in a recording studio). The marketing campaign begins to be developed. Usually the producer, director and star (if important enough) will be involved in creating the marketing strategy. The writer is almost never involved unless he or she is the director, producer or important star.

The studio tests various versions or "cuts" of the film with audiences, which can profoundly affect the marketing strategy and final editing. Sometimes this process leads to more re-shoots.

A release date is set and the marketing campaign begins. There's a buildup to a frenzy of activity consisting of film reviews, celebrity media junkets and a variety of premieres.

Theaters exhibit the film. A film can start in limited release (a small number of screens) or in wide release (more than a thousand screens).

After the theatrical run—which could be from two weeks to one year—the film goes to ancillary markets, including cable television, DVD and free TV.

This is an immense machine involving thousands of people from hundreds of areas of expertise. Now let's look at the steps in this process that most affect you, the screenwriter.

Selling Your Screenplay

It's easier to get someone who knows you or knows someone you know to read your script and/or recommend it and/or buy it. I call this the "six degrees of separation" approach; this theory purports that anyone can be connected to any other person on the planet through a chain of acquaintances that has no more than four intermediaries.[2]

To take advantage of this theory, you must be prepared with various tools, which are covered below.

Write a One-Liner

Write a tight and hard-hitting sentence that grabs a reader's (or listener's) interest. Admittedly, this is not an easy task, but it's certainly an important one to accomplish. You never know when you might have the opportunity to pitch this single sentence to someone who has the power to represent you, refer you to an agent or manager, or option or purchase your screenplay. Commit this one-liner to memory and be ready to spit it out at any given moment.

Write a One-Page Synopsis

How do you turn a 115-page screenplay into a one-page summary? It's not easy but it can—and must—be accomplished before you begin the process of marketing your screenplay to anyone in the entertainment business. No one really wants to read an entire screenplay unless he or she feels it is interesting. That's the goal of the synopsis. You should have already started this process with the treatment you developed at the start of the writing process. To reduce the treatment, start by summarizing paragraphs into one sentence. Do this until you're down to a single page.

Another approach is to summarize each sequence in your screenplay (most screenplays consist of eight to ten major sequences) into one paragraph, then summarize the sequences that make up each act. Do this until you get it down to one page.

Polish by adding "tone"—if it's a comedy, it should read funny; if it's a thriller, it should have a thrilling feel; it it's action, it should be explosive. I can't over-emphasize how important this is.

Create a "Dream" Cast

Whom do you see playing the key roles in your screenplay? Make a list. But be realistic. Everyone wants the big stars du jour, but not everyone can get them. Sometimes it works to make a list of less-obvious actors who may not be big stars but are still recognizable names. Take this step seriously, because it can get an agent or manager jazzed up, especially if they have access to a particular actor through a direct or indirect relationship.

Land a Representative

Let me begin by saying that agents all want to see finished screenplays! It's common to hear writer reps ask "How many screenplays have you written?" because they want to know if you're in it for the long haul.

Sometimes a rep has to pass on a screenplay because he or she already represents one like yours; a second or even third script in a different genre can come in handy in this situation.[3]

Three types of professionals represent screenwriters: agents, managers and entertainment attorneys. The basic difference is that an agent and entertainment attorney can negotiate deals, while a manager, by law, can't. The manager's role in a screenwriter's professional life is generally that of career guidance. How a manager "guides" a writer's career will vary greatly from manager to manager. Just remember, agents and attorneys sell the finished screenplay, while managers help the writer develop the material and get it to a state of commercial readiness.

You'll acquire representation for two primary reasons: (1) you've written a very commercial screenplay or (2) there is a call from the industry—studios executives, producers, directors, important actors—to agents or managers for the type of screenplay you've written. It's as simple as that. If neither of these conditions exists, it's rare to sign a contract. In most cases, the contract only comes when it looks like a sale is imminent. Before that, you may have a "sweetheart" or "hip pocket" deal; this means the screenplay is represented, not the writer.

Finding an agent or manager can be as daunting as writing a screenplay. There's no tried-and-true method for accomplishing this, so try everything. Here are some things you can do.

Write Query Letters

Query letters are considered by many to be a shot in the dark, but because the field is so competitive, you must fire into the abyss as many times as you can in the hopes of hitting something. There are many articles and books on the art and craft of writing the query letter. Essentially, the purpose of the letter is to "hook" readers and make them want to call or meet you, or, better yet, read your screenplay. This one-page letter should represent your writing style and personality.

There are many guides that list writer representatives; perhaps the best known is the *Hollywood Creative Directory: Agents & Managers*. The Internet version updates often. The Writers Guild of America, West maintains a list of agents and managers who are willing to accept unsolicited queries. So keep that one-pager handy and be ready to pitch if someone responds to your query.

Develop a Pitch

Developing an arresting way to tell your screenplay's story is necessary. Cliff Roberts, an agent with the William Morris Agency, says: "Your pitch has to capture lightning in a bottle. It has to fit all the criteria. It has to be a very marketable idea. It has to be something you can completely understand in terms of how you would market it in one or two sentences, and its got to have a title that people understand immediately."[4]

Then you must tell the story in broad strokes and lure the listener in by painting visual images and evoking emotional empathy for the characters. It's almost like story-time for children: you want to their eyes to light up, you want them to laugh when it's funny, gasp when it's unbelievable and fret when it's scary. However, although pitching is an important part of selling your script, there is a reality: for all but the top-level established writers, it makes more sense to bring a finished script to the table.[5]

Still, be prepared to pitch if you're not on that elite list.

Go to Pitch Festivals

These events generally cost money to attend. Look at them in two ways: (1) as a vehicle to practice your pitching to real-life buyers and (2) as a chance to meet people in the entertainment business who may be able to assist you down the line, if not immediately. To find out about these events, read trade publications such as *Daily Variety* and *The Hollywood Reporter*, as well as magazines such as *Creative Screenwriting*, *Scr(i)pt* and *Fade In*. Many entertainment websites publish this information, too.

When you attend, try to match up your screenplay genre with the type of genre the potential buyer has produced in the past or has indicated an interest in.

Sometimes these festivals take the form of luncheons. It's inadvisable to pitch a project that you have not yet written, because more often than not the potential buyer will ask to read the script immediately if he or she is interested.

Most companies attending pitch festivals are smaller or independent companies that do not develop from the idea stage, or pay someone to write a screenplay from its inception, so you should pitch a well-written script—one that has some attachments in the form of actors, director or money.[6] Many of these companies are more interested in small films, primarily quirky dramas. However, more and more, popular genre screenplays are becoming of interest at these events.

Enter Screenwriting Contests

There's a gaggle of this type of contest. The most prestigious is the Nicholl Fellowships in Screenwriting.[7] However, the winning films in this competition are generally not popular genres. You can find listings of various contests by doing a search on the Internet.

Post a Screenplay on the Internet

This is tricky business because you don't know who's looking at your material and your ideas can easily be stolen. Most of these websites charge fees to list your screenplay. Most build in some protection, but still, tread carefully.

Attend Screenwriting Conferences

Each year, there are hundreds of these meetings, running from one day to one week. You can find conferences on the Internet or in popular screenwriting trade magazines. They offer great opportunities for networking.

Use Professional Readers or Script Consultants

These can be story analysts, story editors or script consultants. Some work for studios full time, others freelance. Tread carefully, because the quality of advice you pay for will vary widely, and the prices can get expensive. Ultimately, a reader will do "coverage" on your script by writing a summary. Here are some of the common problems they tend to find in screenplays:

→ The reader is not hooked in the first 5–10 pages
→ The reader does not know what the story is about by page 30 (end of Act One)
→ The script doesn't "feel" like a movie
→ The reader can't visualize stars in the key roles

Admittedly, these big issues go right to the heart of a screenplay. If your script consistently receives these types of remarks from readers, you need to do some major rewriting. Strive to make your screenplay "reader proof." As hard as it is to accept, screenwriters must make the readers' comments go away by addressing them in revisions, since this is the primary gateway for scripts getting into the system.

Networking & Self Promotion

It's important to go where people you want to read your screenplay are, whether these venues are social or professional. You have to be your best promoter, *especially* if you have an agent or manager, because that's the ultimate question that he or she will ask if there's interest. Getting turned down is a reality in the entertainment business, especially for screenwriters. It's helpful to develop a thick skin. If you're told no but the relationship has gone well, try to turn it into an opportunity by opening another door for a future screenplay.

The Standard Release Form

If you do not have an agent, manager or attorney to submit your screenplay, a production company will ask you to sign a standard release form.

"Release forms may make it more difficult for you to sue someone for ripping you off, but such forms may not provide a complete shield," says entertainment attorney Mark Litwak. "If the person who rips you off does so intentionally, they may be liable, regardless of the terms of the release."[8]

Get in the habit of creating a paper trail: keep a calendar of all meetings, write letters confirming specifics of discussions, keep copies of all correspondence and write memos as the records of phone conversations. All of these steps help to prove that the offending party had access to your material. However, the idea is to *prevent* lawsuits, not to win or lose one. As the old saying goes, "Only the lawyers win in litigation."

Copyrights & Registration

You can register your screenplay with the Writers of Guild of America, using their online service. It cost more if you're not a member. You can also register your script at the Library of Congress. The goal here is to give your screenplay an "official" birth date. You should register the screenplay just before taking it public and each time you do a *major* revision after that. You will receive a certificate and the registration is good for ten years.

The Writers Guild of America, West

Go to *www.wga.org* to learn all about this organization. It is the union for screenwriters.

The Screenplay Marketplace by Genre

Why is it important for the screenwriter to understand the importance of marketing? Because few—if any—studios will purchase a screenplay, and ultimately produce it as a film, if the studio doesn't feel it can sell the movie to an identifiable segment of the movie-going public. What that means to you is that the elements in your script must virtually scream the one-sheet movie poster, the casting of bankable actors and the potential for the video market, which includes DVD, and pay and free television sales. Figure 7.1 illustrates the importance of this fact.

Figure 7.1 *Film Economics of Major Studios Releases per Film by Genre, 1996–2003*[9]

DOLLAR FIGURES IN MILLIONS

GENRE	NUMBER OF FILMS	AVERAGE BOX OFFICE	AVERAGE WORLDWIDE	AVERAGE WORLD COST	AVERAGE GROSS PROFIT
Sc-fi/fantasy	62	$96.3	$300.0	$145.8	$154.1
Animation/ fantasy	103	$64.0	$236.1	$120.2	$115.9
Romance	68	$45.5	$121.1	$ 73.3	$ 47.2
Action	193	$61.5	$194.4	$121.9	$ 72.5
Horror	58	$38.4	$102.9	$ 66.3	$ 36.6
Comedy	291	$45.0	$123.0	$ 80.1	$ 42.9
Drama	202	$45.2	$127.4	$ 85.5	$ 41.8
Thriller	85	$43.4	$127.0	$ 89.2	$ 37.7
Western	5	$23.1	$ 70.2	$ 77.9	$ 7.7
TOTAL (average)	1,067	$52.3	$156.8	$ 95.9	$ 60.8

Figure 7.2 *Studio Market Share*[10]

JANUARY 1–DECEMBER 25, 2007

OVERALL GROSS: $9.310 BILLION

RANK	DISTRIBUTOR	MARKET SHARE	TOTAL GROSS*	MOVIES TRACKED	2007 MOVIES**
1	Paramount	15.9%	$1,479.4	20	16
2	Warner Bros.	14.5%	$1,351.0	34	24
3	Buena Vista	13.6%	$1,270.1	21	13
4	Sony / Columbia	13.1%	$1,219.2	28	25
5	Universal	11.6%	$1,076.0	20	8
6	20th Century Fox	10.2%	$945.9	24	16
7	New Line	5.1%	$479.0	17	13
8	Lionsgate	4.0%	$368.1	17	17
9	MGM/UA	3.8%	$354.5	29	19
10	Miramax	1.3%	$121.71	0	8
11	Fox Searchlight	1.2%	$113.7	15	10
12	Rogue Pictures	0.8%	$73.0	3	3

* In millions.
** Number of total movies tracked that were released in 2007.

Writing Is Writing & Selling Is Selling

The hardest hurdle for many screenwriters to overcome is separating the writing process from the selling process. Yes, it's important to write screenplays that will sell. It's equally important to write from the heart and write what excites you. Then, when it's all said and done, look at the marketplace and see if there's a place for your script. The best advice I can give you is to tell yourself continually, "When I'm writing, I'm writing. When I'm selling, I'm selling."

In the end, regardless of genre, you're writing for an audience that, first and foremost, wants to be thoroughly entertained. Everything else, as they say, is icing. Of course, this does not preclude creating a screenplay that appeals to buyers and audiences alike, and that's why it's so important to learn the essential elements of each popular film genre. Both customers expect it.

Finally, writing to genre requirements does not excuse you from needing originality and creativity. You must bring the unexpected to the expected to succeed.

Good luck and good writing!

NOTES

1. Source: Writer's Guild of America, West, 2007 Annual Report.

2. Wikipedia, "Six Degrees of Separation," *http://en.wikipedia.org/wiki/Six_degrees_of_separation* (accessed March 29, 2006).

3. Michael T. Kuciak, "Seven Steps to Getting a Literary Manager," *Scr(i)pt* magazine, July/August 2005, 60.

4. Tom Matthews, "You Hate Pitching, You Have to Do It: Here's How," *Creative Screenwriting* magazine, March/April 2006, 69.

5. David Michael Wharton, "Hollywood Roundtable: Specs, Pitches & Assignments," *Creative Screenwriting* magazine, March/April 2005, 57.

6. Susan Bedusa and Douglas Tirola, "Speed Pitching: How to Pitch at a Festival," *Scr(i)pt* magazine, January/February 2005, 58.

7. For further information contact:
Nicholl Fellowships in Screenwriting
The Academy Foundation
1313 N. Vine Street
Hollywood, California 90028-8107
(310) 247-3010
nicholl@oscars.org

8. Steve Ryfle, "License to Steal?" *Creative Screenwriting* magazine, January/February 2006, 39.

9. Robert Marich, *Marketing to Moviegoers: A Handbook of Strategies Used by Major Studios and Independents* (Oxford: Focal Press of Elsevier, 2005), 216.

10. Source: *www.boxofficemojo.com/studio.*

Appendix A

Character Development Template

Full Name
_____

Dramatic Role: Hero(ine)? Villain(ess)? Sidekick(s) (male or female)? Henchmen (women)?
_____

PSYSIOLOGICAL PROFILE

Sex
_____

Age
_____

General Appearance
_____

General Health
_____

Abnormalities (defects, if any)
_____

SOCIOLOGICAL PROFILE

Race & Religion
_____

Class Status
_____

Home Life (past and present, and the influence of it)
_____

Education
_____

Occupation & Abilities
_____

Key Relationships
_____

Politics (views on current important issues)
_____

Hobbies
_____

PSYCHOLOGICAL PROFILE

Sex Life
_____

Ethics, Values & Moral Standards
_____

Drives & Ambitions
_____

Frustrations & Disappointments
_____

Temperament
_____

IQ
_____

General Attitude
_____

Complexes (if any)
_____

Qualities Important to the Story
_____

How the Audience Feels about This Character
_____

Appendix B

---●----------------------➤

Action-Adventure Worksheet

The High-Concept Premise
_____

The Theme
_____

The Hero with a Strong Goal
_____

The Villain with a Strong Goal
_____

Key Pivotal Characters (*Buddies and Henchmen*)
_____

The Villain's Plan
_____

The Hero's Basic Story
_____

The Hero's Love Story
_____

THE EIGHT MAJOR ACTION SEQUENCES

Act One
_____

1.
_____

2.
_____

3.
_____

Act Two

_____

4.

_____

5.

_____

6.

_____

7.

_____

Act Three

_____

8.

_____

Appendix C

Thriller Worksheet

The "Intriguing" Working Title

_____

The Sub-Genre

_____

The Theme

_____

The Setting

_____

THE CAST OF CHARACTERS

Protagonist with a Strong Goal (*Amateur, Semi-Pro, Private Detective or Police*)

_____

Antagonist and/or Villain with a Strong Goal (*Desperate, Average or Seemingly Invincible*)

_____

The Femme Fatale

_____

The Ingénue

_____

List of Suspects (*at least three, one a red herring*)

_____

_____

_____

_____

The High-Concept Premise

_____

The McGuffin

_____

The Apparent Story

_____

The Real Story

_____

The Love Story Subplot

_____

Appendix D

Science-Fiction-Fantasy Worksheet

The "Fascinating" Working Title
_____

The Sub-Genre
_____

The Contemporary Problem Theme
_____

The Unique World (Setting)
_____

THE CAST OF CHARACTERS

Protagonist with a Strong Goal
_____

Antagonist and/or Villain with a Strong Goal
_____

Key Pivotal Characters
_____

_____

_____

_____

_____

_____

The High-Concept Premise
_____

THE FIVE ESSENTIAL ELEMENTS

The Threat

The Expert

The Emotional Jeopardy

The Demonstration

The Lesson

The Basic Story

The Love Story Subplot

Appendix D

The "Foreboding" Working Title

_____

The Sub-Genre

_____

The Theme (a form of self annihilation and fear)

_____

The Setting

_____

THE CAST OF CHARACTERS

The Hero or Heroine with a Strong Goal

_____

The "Monster" with a Strong Goal (*Human, Unhuman, Human/Unhuman*)

_____

_____

The High-Concept Premise

_____

The Story (*the "nightmare"*)

_____

_____

The Love Story Subplot (*the emotional core*)

_____

_____